Ellen Glasgow

MODERN LITERATURE SERIES

GENERAL EDITOR: Philip Winsor

In the same series:

(*continued on last page of book*)

ELLEN GLASGOW

Marcelle Thiébaux

FREDERICK UNGAR PUBLISHING CO.
NEW YORK

Copyright© 1982 by Frederick Ungar Publishing Co.,
Inc.
Printed in the United States of America

Library of Congress Cataloging in Publication Data

Thiébaux, Marcelle.
  Ellen Glasgow.

  (Modern literature series)
  Bibliography: p.
  Includes index.
  1. Glasgow, Ellen Anderson Gholson, 1873–1945—
Criticism and interpretation.   I. Title.   II. Series.
PS3513.L34Z9   813'.52   81–70128
ISBN 0–8044–2872–7   AACR2

Acknowledgments

I wish to express my gratitude to Josephine Glasgow Clark of Richmond, Virginia, for so graciously sharing with me her memories of her aunt, Ellen Glasgow. My deep thanks are also due to Edgar E. MacDonald, Editor of the *Ellen Glasgow Newsletter*, for his most generous advice. Among those colleagues and editors whose help and criticism proved valuable, I would like particularly to thank Elaine Hoffman Baruch, James Hafley, Lina Mainiero and Philip Winsor. To members of the staff of St. John's University who assisted in the preparation of the manuscript, Jean Belmont and Charlotte Johnson, I am very grateful. Special appreciation goes to the curators and the resources of the libraries where I worked: The St. John's University Library, The Columbia University Library, The Alderman Library of The University of Virginia, The American Academy and Institute of Arts and Letters, and The New York Public Library, both for its extensive collection and for providing a desk in The Frederick Lewis Allen Room.

To Cameron

Contents

Chronology

1853	July 4: Marriage of Anne Jane Gholson and Francis Thomas Glasgow.
1873	April 22: Birth of Ellen Anderson Glasgow at 101 East Cary Street, Richmond, Virginia.
1888	Family moves to 1 West Main Street, Glasgow's home for the rest of her life.
1889	Début at St. Cecilia Ball in Charleston, South Carolina.
1893	October 27: Mother dies.
1894	Suicide of brother-in-law and mentor, Walter McCormack.
1895	First story, "A Woman of To-morrow," published.
1896	First European travel.
1897	*The Descendant* published.
1898	*Phases of an Inferior Planet* published.
1900	*The Voice of the People* published.
1902	*The Battle-Ground* published.
	The Freeman and Other Poems published.
1904	*The Deliverance* published.
1905	"Gerald B—," Glasgow's first love, dies.
1906	*The Wheel of Life* published.
1907	Engagement, eventually broken, to the Reverend Frank Ilsley Paradise.
1908	*The Ancient Law* published.
1909	*The Romance of a Plain Man* published.
	April 7: Suicide of brother, Frank Glasgow.
1910	Anne Virginia Bennett comes to the Glasgow household.

1911   *The Miller of Old Church* published.
            Glasgow elected first vice-president of the
            Richmond Society for the Prevention of Cru-
            elty to Animals.
            August 19: Cary, Glasgow's sister, dies.
            Moves to New York to live intermittently
            until 1915.

1913   Portrait painted by Prince Pierre Troubetz-
            koy.
            Virginia published.

1916   January 29: Father dies. Glasgow returns to
            Richmond.
            Life and Gabriella published.
            Easter Sunday meeting with Henry W. An-
            derson.

1917   July 19: Engagement, eventually broken, to
            Henry Anderson.

1918   July 3: Takes overdose of sleeping pills after
            evening with Henry Anderson.

1919   *The Builders* published.

1920   December 4: Elected to Phi Beta Kappa at
            the College of William and Mary.

1922   *One Man in His Time* published.

1923   *The Shadowy Third and Other Stories* pub-
            lished.

1924   Glasgow elected president of the Richmond
            Society for the Prevention of Cruelty to Ani-
            mals.

1925   *Barren Ground* published.

1926   *The Romantic Comedians* published.

1929   *They Stooped to Folly* published.

1929–1933   *Old Dominion* edition of eight novels ap-
            pears.

1930   June 10: Awarded honorary degree of doctor
            of letters, University of North Carolina.

1931   October 23–24: Southern Writers Confer-
            ence, organized by Glasgow, takes place at
            the University of Virginia, Charlottesville.

1932   *The Sheltered Life* published.
            Elected to the National Institute of Arts and
            Letters.

1933   Embittered over failure to get expected Pu-
            litzer Prize for *The Sheltered Life.*

1935   *Vein of Iron* published.

1935   September: *Vein of Iron* is made Book-of-
              the-Month-Club selection.
1937   Last European travel.
1938   April 29: Awarded honorary degree of doctor
              of laws, University of Richmond.
              June 6: Awarded honorary degree of doctor
              of laws, Duke University.
              Virginia Edition of twelve novels appears.
              December: Elected to the American Acad-
              emy of Arts and Letters.
1939   June 5: Awarded honorary degree of doctor
              of laws, College of William and Mary.
              December: First heart attack.
1940   November 15: Awarded Howells medal for
              fiction by American Academy of Arts and
              Letters.
1941   *In This Our Life* published.
              April 5: Given *Saturday Review of Literature*
              award for distinguished service to American
              literature.
1942   May 5: Awarded Pulitzer Prize for fiction for
              1941, for *In This Our Life*.
              Warner Brothers film of *In This Our Life*
              released.
              Awarded Southern Authors prize.
1943   *A Certain Measure* published.
1945   November 21: Dies at age of seventy-two at
              1 West Main Street, Richmond.
1954   *The Woman Within,* her autobiography,
              published.
1958   *Letters of Ellen Glasgow* published.
1963   *The Collected Stories of Ellen Glasgow* pub-
              lished.
1966   *Beyond Defeat* published.

Introduction

Ellen Glasgow was a writer of the South, notably of Virginia. Her allegiance was fervent: "I am a Virginian in every drop of my blood and pulse of my heart." Her chosen subject was Virginia's social history, and as the first writer of the modern South she gave literary definition to the region in its post-Reconstruction period. She recreates a richly textured country scene, a landscape she populates with homely figures. Her rustics wisecrack in the back room of the general store. Her folk, endowed with fortitude, grow ruggedly out of the earth, their identities often apparent in their names—Oakley, Burr, Spade, Berry, Bottom. The land becomes a metaphor for her literary art. "Great novels must have roots." "My social history had sprung from a special soil." "I saw a fertile, an almost virgin, field ahead of me."[1]

The decay of the Southern city, with its concomitant industrial growth, is also her business. She writes about factories and railroads, their smells, strikes, and financial crises, the stresses of politics shared by patricians and the new men of the rising middle class. She ironically examines Richmond as a center of remembered elegance, saturated in its history and faithful to its traditions, manners, and patriarchal code. Her upper-class women, whether victims or fiery hearts, embody the cult of the lady in its de-

cline. Other women characters are doughty folk heroines. In all cases Glasgow understands female anger
and the woman's plight. Among the men, her rakes,
generals, and statesmen represent the dregs of a seigneurial agrarian aristocracy, dispossessed by the Civil
War but still imbued with courtesy and rhetoric. In
many "the spirit of adventure had disintegrated into
an evasive idealism."[2] Their names come from the
annals of Virginia history: Bland, Blair, Burwell,
Wythe, Culpeper. Her blacks, affectionately portrayed, are on the whole stereotypical in their
humor, loyalty, and easy-going ways. Glasgow strove
for a hierarchical literary construct of Virginia life as
it was and was becoming. James Branch Cabell called
her work a "large panorama of the customs and fail-
ings and virtues of the State of Virginia." Maxwell
Geismar remarked: "Her novels are among the best
sources of information on the Southern mind just
because we can read in them the imprint of primary
cultural myths on a perceptive and sophisticated talent."[3]

And yet Glasgow resisted being termed a Southern writer. She thanked reviewers for saying it
wasn't so. Her subject, she maintained, was human
nature in the South, not Southern nature. She wished
"to escape . . . from the provincial into the universal."[4] Her resistance to being labeled a regional
writer made her force her vital sense of place into a
significant scheme. She felt she needed a theory, an
ideology, and much of her writing bears signs of the
strain. Allen Tate believed that Glasgow's distraction
of her creative ability into "propaganda," her com-
pulsive thesis of "Progress," spoiled her novels.[5] An
autodidact, Glasgow had steeped herself in theories
of biological and social evolution that she applied to
her fiction. She believed that the best qualities of the

aristocratic tradition in the South would fuse with the finest energies of the folk, while the worst of both classes would die off. Past, present, and future would be interconnected by some evolutionary ideal of progress. Her system would maintain the continuity of history while representing hope for perpetual future improvement.

This theoretical bent of Glasgow's often led her to write with her eye not freshly on the object and to sacrifice felt life to a schematic view of human nature, society, and history. One unfortunate result of her method was an "oversimplification of the historical process," in which characters tend to be rigidly classified as Old South or New South.[6] Assigned to their periods and subject to historical determinism, they become distorted and lose fleshly credibility. Her thriving protagonists are often racially selected stereotypes. Glasgow's predilection for judiciously mating old-blooded patricians with fresh-blooded plain people has led some readers to discern allegory in her novels. Female characters often seem to stand for aspects of the South: some are graceful but ruined, others sturdy and undefeated. By insisting on an ideology of Southern progress, Glasgow drove her talent against the grain. The harm to her writing became more evident when she found it hard to have faith in human perfectibility but continued to voice an optimism to which she was ideologically committed.

In writing of the better social order to which the South would evolve, Glasgow had to assume that the past was in some ways flawed. She rejected the sentimental literature that had celebrated the Old South, the "moonlight and magnolia" plantation romances.[7] Glasgow was not alone in this view. Of the writing of the period, that "desouthernized Southerner," Mark

Twain, had also deplored the "wordy, windy, flowery, 'eloquence' " that persisted in the South.[8] Glasgow explained it:

After the War, pursued by the dark furies of Reconstruction, the mind of the South was afflicted with a bitter nostalgia. From this homesickness for the past there flowered, as luxuriantly as fireweed in burned places, a mournful literature of commemoration.[9]

This literature was "deficient in blood and irony, and true, not to experience, but to the attitude of evasive idealism." Hating the "moribund convention," she would "revolt against the formal, the false, the affected, the sentimental, and the pretentious in Southern writing."

A self-styled rebel armed with social theories, Glasgow undertook her hard reexamination of the decadent Old South thinking to expose the so-called 'shabbiness' of chivalry. Once launched, however, she was unable to maintain her position; her mockery became tinted with more affection than she intended. The landed, feudal, family-centered society of her forebears, she decided, had left something of value. She ended by praising the patricians' statesmanship and learning, preservation of art, generosity and altruism, willingness to dare brilliantly for an ideal, and respect for manners as the basis of morality. Alfred Kazin found her both a satirist of Virginia and an old-fashioned, loyal traditionalist. "A little too much has been made, I think, of Ellen Glasgow's revolt against the formalized tradition of the Old South," James Cabell had written: "As a person, she has very sensibly fallen in with that formalized and amiable luxurious manner of living to which she was born."[10]

Even while claiming to lay bare the ills that the Old South had bequeathed to the New, Glasgow

grew reluctant to probe these. A sickened upper
class clinging to its haunted past, the family as a
hotbed of ills, the rivalry between parents and children and between the sexes, racial tension, the earth-
iness of poor whites and the arrogance of the landed
old families—all these she broached, but broached
only. Younger Southern writers picked up where she
left off. Those who "arrested the reading and theatrical world with the tragic intensity of the inner life
and the social drama of the South, . . . could find
scarcely a theme that Ellen Glasgow had wholly neglected."[11] The subjects treated by Tennessee Williams and William Faulkner can be found within the
more genteel limits of Glasgow's novels.

Louis D. Rubin, Jr. considers Glasgow's role
"transitional":

Midway between the old romance and the latter-day realism she stands. . . . She occupies a position midway between
those writers of the South's long Victorian twilight . . . and
the post–World War I novelists of the Renascence,
[Thomas] Wolfe, [Robert Penn] Warren, above all [Wil-
liam] Faulkner—a writer whose work she thoroughly disliked.[12]

For she had no patience with the fiction of her
younger contemporaries. She came to loathe those
literary characters she called the "half-wits, and
whole idiots, and nymphomaniacs, and paranoiacs,
and rake-hells in general, that populate the modern
literary South."[13] Some temperamental restraint and
an essentially romantic sensibility prevented her
from carrying the themes she initiated to their dark
and necessary conclusions. She touched on crime,
alienation, and despair but did not examine their
deeper consequences. Her people emerge from har-
rowing experiences with inconsistent, cheerful optimism. Her novels usually contain, as Cabell re-

marked, "the last cry of romance" and close with "a
light in the sky or in somebody's eyes." Glasgow,
after "supplying her Virginians with trials and de-
feats and irrevocable losses, yet almost always manage[s] to end, somehow, upon this brave note of re-
cording her people's renovated belief in a future during which everything will turn out quite splen-
didly."[14]

Among the problems about which Glasgow tried
to be optimistic was the plight of women. Within her
announced theme of Virginia social history, her
documented commentary on women's lives forms an
important subtheme. Her female characters usually
have a deeper felt life than her men. Cabell noted
this preoccupation; he thought she had done a "complete natural history of the Southern gentlewoman,
with every attendant feature of her lair and general
habitat most accurately rendered." Recent studies
single out this aspect of her work.[15]

The freeing of women from their old constraints
raises moral questions for Glasgow. She likes to show
the effects of wars, from the Civil War to World War
II. War makes the superior woman tougher and more
competent, whereas the shallow woman irresponsi-
bly accepts its attendant sexual liberation. Suffrage as
a public issue occupies Glasgow, although she had
mixed feelings about women's voting and talked
confidently about their influence. She disparages
young would-be suffragists. Those who loudly insist
on their rights without acknowledging their duties
are not her favorites.

She generally divides the nineteenth-century
"womanly woman" from the woman who after the
turn of the century managed to extricate herself
from Victorian genteel codes. Usually there is a conflict or failure of understanding between the two.
Her own ambivalence surfaces, for she had an emo-

tional preference for the former, the gracious women of her mother's generation. Although she was indignant over the repression and exploitation they often endured, she deeply admired their "fragrant charm" and regretted the modern woman's loss of that quality. The more autonomy enjoyed by the younger generation, the more Glasgow was apt to deplore their seeming hardness. Not really in touch with the young, she makes her girlish characters too often appear shallow, even degraded. Glasgow never quite could abandon a belief in traditional femininity. Her ideal was the responsible, intelligent woman who had something to occupy her mind yet who still retained an aura of Victorian grace and a ladylike dignity about sex.

In addition to the general distinction between the two generations, Glasgow's fictions contain a great range of female types in various roles—daughters, sisters, fiancées, mistresses, wives, mothers, grandmothers. Society nearly always places them in embattled confrontations with men. Matrimony is treated negatively. Some romantic heroines seem hopeful as they look forward to marriage; married heroines are disillusioned. Glasgow understands how the patriarchal system harms women, either making them suffer or so morally distorting them that they maltreat others, like her tyrannic lady invalids. Others are broken by or resentfully rage against the vain and treacherous male.

The most common injury that men inflict on women is to betray their love. Rarely do Glasgow's women find authentic happiness in loving or exult in joyous sexuality. Those who are deprived of love have predatory sexual dreams. But women to whom sexual love is available tend to exclaim with repugnance over kissing, touching, and fondling. Lovemaking offers little pleasure, and women pay dearly for indulging in it. Glasgow tended to look upon the sexually active woman with suspicion and even to judge her as weak, cold, and manipulative. Being "finished with love" is the ideal many of her heroines strive for, although they do not always sound convincing about it.

If relationships between men and women are usually spoiled by masculine treachery, where then could perfect companionship be found? In her own life Glasgow gave her unwavering devotion to women: her mother, her sister, and the woman who was her lifelong companion. Her letters reveal an affectionate correspondence with other women writers. When, for instance, Marjorie Kinnan Rawlings visited her and then wrote of her dream of holding Glasgow's tiny hand in hers to protect her from the cold, Glasgow's response is noteworthy for its generous ardor:

[Your letter] brought a thrilling sense of friendship and sympathy. . . . Ever since you came to see me, so strong and warm and vital, I have felt very near to you.[16]

In several of the novels there are women characters who have given up love to find a consolation in each other's company that is said to be tenderer than any relationship with husband or lover. Despite the pointed comparison, it does not seem likely that Glasgow meant lesbian sexuality, for she parenthetically informs the reader in *They Stooped to Folly* that the women share a pure and "sinless" friendship. In *The Miller of Old Church,* she acknowledges the existence of an unwritten women's life of which her work is a partial document:

The relation of woman to man was dwarfed suddenly by an understanding of the relation of woman to woman. Deeper

than the dependence of sex, simpler, more natural, closer
to the earth, as though it still drew its strength from the
soil, . . . the need of woman for woman was not written in
the songs nor in the histories of men, but in the neglected
and frustrated lives, which the songs and the histories of
men had ignored.

Apart from women's affectional lives, Glasgow
deals with the question of how they work to survive.
She shows pity or contempt for those who wait for a
man to take care of them or who preach such passivity. Women of grit, genius, or beauty may be able to
make their way in a male world. But what of average
women? Glasgow gives particular attention to their
quandary, how they prepare their minds and organize their lives. Except for a few, like her artist heroines, they stoically do the usual feminine things—
housework, dressmaking, selling in a shop, teaching
school (badly), decorating, nursing, or serving as
lady's companion or secretary. They struggle to retain their center. Often they hope for love as well.
Despite all that Glasgow would want to say to the
contrary, her women are never so finished with the
idea of love as they think they ought to be. Glasgow's
views on women are filled with telling conflicts that
belie the optimism she seeks to affirm. Both her
major and her minor novels offer a rewarding discourse on the conditions, choices, and neuroses of
women as she saw them and contain copious indict-
ments of the patriarchal social controls as well.

In sum, Glasgow renders the life of the Virginia
region at a particular epoch, with its terrain, history,
and manners. She satirizes the humors and the grotesque perpetrators of social deceits. A New Southern writer, she forecasts the modernist crisis that was
more thoroughly explored by her successors.
Throughout her fiction, as a dark and churning un-

dercurrent, runs a discourse of critical feminist importance that is all the more valuable for the unresolved conflicts it betrays. Her irony ranges from the delicate to the tragic. By its means she confronted obliquely and through sardonic laughter the behavior that disguised the menaces of life.

1

○○○○○○○○○○○○○○○○○○○○○○○○○○○○○○○

"The Many Tragedies of My Life"

When Ellen Glasgow's autobiography appeared nine years after her death, friends were surprised to read that her life had been "a long tragedy." This witty, brilliantly sociable Southern grande dame of their acquaintance, who loved laughter and lived elegantly, did not match the morbid self-image she projected in *The Woman Within.* There she confessed herself stalked all her life by mishaps, depressions, terrors, and illnesses. The onslaught in youth of her isolating deafness aggravated the unhappiness that was her grim secret: "That I, who was winged for flying, should be wounded and caged!" To mask her pain, she cultivated "the ironic mood, the smiling pose" that she held on to "without a break or a change, for almost forty years."[1]

Much of what Glasgow wrote about herself stresses her divided spirit. Brought up as a belle and presented to society in white flounced organdie with a rose in her hair, she chose to revolt against ladylike tradition and to compete in the hard arena of art. She strove for realism but could not relinquish the romantic. A skeptic, she intellectually renounced orthodox religion, yet she felt she was a believer in her heart. Fascinated by her own genealogy, for which she gathered voluminous notes, she thought of her personality as split from conception:

I had the misfortune . . . to inherit a long conflict of types, for my father was a descendant of Scottish Calvinists and my mother was a perfect flower of the Tidewater, in Virginia.[2]

Her father was Francis Thomas Glasgow (1829–1916), head of the armaments factory called the Tredegar Iron Works in Richmond. For Glasgow he was always the iron father with his "iron will," his "vein of iron." A board member of the State Penitentiary, an elder of the Presbyterian Church, he had "laid hold of the eternal and invisible with a strong grasp."[3] His dour forebears, descended from the Camerons of Glasgow, settled in the western Virginia frontier in 1766. Glasgow's gentle mother, Anne Gholson Glasgow, came of a family of jurists claiming an older ancestry from among Virginia's English settlers.

Glasgow was born on April 22, 1873, in a house at 101 East Cary Street in Richmond. She was the eighth of ten children, four boys and six girls. An eleventh was stillborn. By then her mother was "worn . . . to a beautiful shadow" by her too-frequent pregnancies and the hardships of having lived through the Civil War and Reconstruction.[4] Her mother's emotional breakdown in her later years and her distraught murmuring throughout the night darkened Glasgow's childhood. She saw her parents as incompatible and developed an antipathy toward her father for his unbending authority, his devotion to a God who "savored the strong smoke of blood sacrifice," his invoking St. Paul to his daughters, his philandering with the black maids, and his lack of feeling for animals that Glasgow and her mother tenderly loved. He was "more patriarchal than paternal."[5] Yet the Calvinist "vein of iron" she attributed to his ancestry is a phrase that recurs approvingly in more than half of her novels.[6]

A sickly child who was not expected to live, Glasgow got a reprieve from formal schooling. At home she read the novels of Sir Walter Scott. With her beloved Mammy Lizzie she made up stories and at seven wrote her first, "Only a Daisy." It summed up her sense of separateness: A lover chooses the simple daisy from among more beautiful garden flowers. The idea persisted. Glasgow's heroines are usually plain but strong, whereas lovelier women turn out to be unworthy. Childhood summers were spent at Jerdone Castle, a vast Louisa County estate thirty miles northwest of Richmond; it provided the old plantation setting for some of her fictions.

When Glasgow was fifteen the family moved to the 1841 Greek Revival mansion on the corner of West Main and Foushee Streets, the house in which she would live until her death. In this house she knew a measure of happiness, as well as "the many tragedies of my life." One of the latter was her tormenting deafness at twenty that would drive her to seek out countless cures without avail. Certain characters in her novels suffer a "rustling void," or a "soundless confusion which vibrated without and within," conditions that evidently reflected this malady. She felt the house to be haunted by "ghosts"—sad childhood memories, her mother's nervous illness and death, the deaths of an infant brother and a brother of sixteen, a withdrawn brother's suicide "sacrificed to [her father's] iron will,"[7] and the wasting away through cancer of her beloved married sister, Cary, after her husband's suicide.

That husband, Walter McCormack, had been an important influence in Glasgow's self-education. Given to solitary reading, Glasgow had enjoyed the novels of Fielding, Dickens, Meredith, Balzac, and Maupassant. Thomas Hardy, her older contemporary, was a novelist she frankly emulated. Her broth-

er-in-law McCormack was a sensitive, brooding intellectual who introduced her to the works of philosophers, naturalists, economists, and political theorists.
Under his guidance she eagerly read Ernst Haeckel,
August Weismann, Edward Gibbon, John Stuart Mill,
Walter Bagehot, Herbert Spencer, Thomas Huxley,
and, most notably, Charles Darwin.[8] When Cary and
Walter gave her a subscription to the Mercantile Library in New York she found a world of ideas opening to her.

The effect of this youthful reading is discernible
in all Glasgow's writing. It gave Glasgow a vocabu-
lary for treating men and women as biological and
social beings. The earliest novels somewhat crudely
incorporate her new learning—book titles, epi-
graphs, and scientific metaphors from the fields of
electricity, biology, and chemistry. Darwin's ideas of
natural selection as set forth in *The Origin of Species*
influenced much nineteenth century literature and
would permanently shape Glasgow's outlook.

According to Darwin, forms of life are plastic; in
the struggle for existence species are continually de-
veloping to adjust to new conditions. Those forms
that cannot change die off; the adaptable or the
fittest survive. Glasgow used these theories to de-
scribe the rivalries between persons of different social or genetic backgrounds, often between men and
women who labor under the stress of history, environment, or emotion. Those of good stock and
"fibre" (a favorite word of hers), inheriting large
brows or jaws or the inner "vein of iron," are survivors. Those incapable of adjusting are portrayed as
rigid comic grotesques or as pathetic or tragic victims. Writing about the period after the Civil War,
Glasgow wanted to show that class structures could
change, as decadent aristocrats and feckless simple
folk alike must succumb while the energetic would

prevail. Her strong women, made hard by circumstance, are always genetically superior. Throughout her work Glasgow plays variations upon the theme of natural selection; even when muted it is never wholly absent from her thinking.

Glasgow tore up her first novel, a 400-page manuscript called *Sharp Realities*. She had tried, at eighteen, to place it with a New York agent; he demanded a fifty-dollar fee and then pursued her around his office in an attempt to kiss her with his "red and juicy lips."[9] It may have been this experience that shook her confidence. The occasion of her first published novel in 1897 was clouded by the recent deaths of her mother and her mentor McCormack. Certain of her high-strung suicidal or murdered male characters resemble McCormack, found mysteriously dead in a New York hotel. Glasgow dedicated *The Descendant* to him. It bore marks of his erudite influence and of the books he had given her.

Another phase of Glasgow's reading was in works of mysticism and philosophy: Plotinus, Marcus Aurelius, St. Francis of Assisi, the Bhagavad-Gita, the Upanishads, the Buddhist Suttas, and Schopenhauer.[10] She felt they offered consolation; aspects of their thought also found their way into her novels. This tendency of the young novelist to flaunt her learning had to be tamed. Glasgow was fortunate in her friend and literary advisor, Walter Hines Page. Then an associate editor of the *Atlantic Monthly*, later a partner in the new firm of Doubleday Page & Company, Page had an interest in Southern writers. He urged Glasgow not to put so much "metaphysics" into her fiction and not to waste energy on poems and short stories. Novels would be her best work. He helped her personally, finding an apartment in New York for her and serving as a confidant to whom she could write of her worries and eagerness for fame.

Glasgow established her life as a woman of letters at the house at 1 West Main, with frequent visits to New York. She wrote nine novels between 1897 and 1911. Her household grew smaller, reduced by departures, marriages, and deaths, until it included Glasgow, her father, Cary, and two other sisters, Rebe and Emily, who eventually married. A trained nurse named Anne Virginia Bennett was engaged for Cary. When Cary died in 1911 Glasgow went to New York to stay intermittently until 1915, when she returned to Richmond. Anne Virginia stayed on for the next thirty-odd years, first to nurse old Mr. Glasgow and then as companion, secretary, and nurse to Glasgow until the author's death. So much did Miss Bennett seem a part of the family that Mr. Glasgow proposed marriage to her when he was over eighty. He was refused, but the incident heightened Glasgow's dislike of her father. Some of her irritability toward him provoked her brother to compare her and her sisters to King Lear's daughters.

Despite her bouts of depression, her deafness, and the family ghosts, Glasgow's life was full and did not lack pleasures. She had her work, which was uppermost. She produced a book about every two or three years. In addition, there were her travels, her interests, her many friends and professional acquaintances, the men she loved, and her cherished animals.

Glasgow went to France, Scotland, and England in 1896, just before her first novel appeared. Between 1896 and 1937 she made numerous crossings of the Atlantic, visiting in addition Egypt, Greece, Turkey, Italy, and Switzerland. In England she saw the elderly Thomas Hardy (both of them were dog lovers). She visited Joseph Conrad, John Galsworthy, and Arnold Bennett. In America she went often to

New York. She maintained an apartment on Central Park West, and in later years stayed at the Chatham and at the Hotel Weylin. She admitted in an interview that the city's "psychological atmosphere of rush troubles me."[11] But New York had a special place in her writings: It meant freedom, exile, squalor, and disorder. It was the place to which her heroines went when unmarried and pregnant, where they could be artists, where they found exhilarating work or threatening sexual opportunities. In fiction set in New York, mistresses and divorces were also possible.

Vacationing to escape Southern summers, Glasgow headed north to Maine, Cape Cod, the Adirondacks, and Quebec. During the last ten years of her life her chauffeur drove her regularly to a tranquil Maine coastal village called Castine. There her niece, Josephine Glasgow Clark, and Miss Bennett managed the household while Glasgow gave herself over to "work, walk, rest, drive, never anything else, and almost complete isolation."[12] Before her books earned money, her oldest brother, Arthur Graham Glasgow, a successful engineer living in London, readily defrayed medical and travel expenses.

Glasgow's active interest in the woman's suffrage movement began in 1909 and lasted about four years. She marched in London and in Richmond. Together with her sister and women friends she helped organize the Virginia League for Woman Suffrage. She spoke for the cause in Richmond and Norfolk. She gave interviews and articles to the papers, where she expressed her view that woman, responding to "man's ideal of her," had "denied her own humanity." The passivity of women, she felt, was not an innate quality but an acquired characteristic, one that would ultimately be cast off. Woman suffrage, she stated, was as inevitable as evolution.

Generally, however, Glasgow preferred to deal artistically with the questions raised by the women's movement rather than through direct political statement or activism. She was willing to consider her poem "The Call" in *Colliers Magazine* in 1912 to be her "contribution to the cause," but her feminist convictions really lie in her fiction, where women emerge as morally strong. A certain ambivalence about campaigning suffragists surfaces in her 1909 novel *The Romance of a Plain Man* (discussed in Chapter 5). Her final thoughts on the subject seem to be those in *The Woman Within,* where she declares that "so long as the serpent continues to crawl on the ground the primary influence of woman will remain indirect."[13]

An ever increasing circle of friends and acquaintances absorbed much of Glasgow's energies, although uncharitable observers hinted that she chose them on the basis of whether they said kind things about her writing. At various times she entertained, or visited, or corresponded with writers and critics such as Mary Johnston, Amélie Rives, Marjorie Kinnan Rawlings, Howard Mumford Jones, Carl Van Vechten, Allen Tate, Stark Young, Van Wyck Brooks, and Carl Van Doren. Probably none was so important to her work, however, as the Richmond writer James Branch Cabell.[14]

Writing of their close friendship of forty-seven years, Cabell claimed that he knew her "more thoroughly and more comprehendingly . . . than did any other human being during the last twenty years of her living."[15] He saw her candidly with her foibles and strengths—her great capacity for charm, her maliciously entertaining tongue, her devotion to her craft, her thirst for fame, her unhappiness. Cabell and Glasgow microscopically read each other's work. Each dedicated books to the other. Each agreed to review the other's books. As a critic of her writing,

Cabell gave Glasgow counsel and encouragement.

A coolness arose between them, however, stemming from a disagreement on just how much Cabell did contribute to her work. In a favorable review of *Barren Ground,* Cabell observed that, taken together, Glasgow's books amounted to "a portrayal of all social and economic Virginia since the War Between the States."[16] Glasgow later claimed that planning her work thus as a deliberate unity had been her own idea. Indeed, in an early letter to her editor she had spoken of "a series of Virginia novels."[17] Cabell ruefully believed that he had been the first to discern the sweeping nature of the design and that Glasgow had not shown him recognition. Cabell also assisted in the editing of her prefaces for the Virginia Edition of her works in 1937 and 1938, later collected in a separate volume as *A Certain Measure* (1943), a title he suggested. So too with her last novel, *In This Our Life* (1941). Seriously ailing, she sought advice from Cabell, who visited her daily, reading, correcting, revising, encouraging. Their friendship continued until Glasgow's death. But when her posthumous autobiography resuscitated old homosexual and other scandals about the youthful Cabell, he put his injured feelings into print. In all, he felt he had not been sufficiently valued.[18]

Despite their intimacy, Cabell and Glasgow were not romantically involved. She had many male friends, perhaps lovers, although Cabell wrote to her near the end of her life:

With your great zest for life, it is dreadful to think of you as a virgin, but your books offer almost irrefutable testimony to the fact, unless indeed your Virginian ladihood has stepped in and caused you to become reticent.[19]

The "testimony" is offered by Glasgow's heroines, with their repugnance for physical closeness, and by the penalties exacted for sexuality in all her work.

Glasgow often said that she was "unfitted for marriage."[20] Her deafness and her work provided some excuse. She also had a jaundiced view of her parents' married life. Throughout the novels, acid satire and outright humor generally characterize her own observations of matrimony. Yet she had several flirtations, some serious relationships, and at least two long engagements.

She calls her first love "Gerald B—" in her autobiography, a married man she saw in New York and Switzerland between 1899 and 1900. His death drove her to a brief period of withdrawal, and she took solace in reading mystical philosophy. She wrote *The Wheel of Life* (1906) in this period. At thirty-three she embarked on an "experimental" three-year engagement to the handsome Reverend Frank Ilsley Paradise, whom she had met in the Adirondacks. He was a frequent guest in Richmond. But apparently she did not admire his religious temper, or his poetry, which she tore up and burned. Years later when Paradise married and left the ministry, they corresponded again with pleasant feelings on both sides. Other close relationships seemed to verge upon love. Glasgow corresponded with and visited Dr. Pearce Bailey (1865–1922), a distinguished co-founder of the Neurological Institute in New York. He had an interest in connections between psychology and literature, and their friendship had facets that were both professional and personal. Sir Hugh Walpole (1884–1941), the British novelist, came to America as a lecturer in 1920 and was generously received at 1 West Main. Friendship ripened into affection. Even Miss Bennett liked him; and Glasgow named her adored Sealyham puppy, Jeremy, for a character in one of his novels. But Walpole became wasp-tongued and saw in her "a fierce clutching of her literary reputation."[21] Their ten-year correspondence grew sporadic and ceased.

Glasgow's deepest, most enduring relationship was with the lawyer Henry W. Anderson, whom she called "Harold S—" in her autobiography. The son of a physician, Anderson came of a good Virginia family whose fortunes had suffered reverses after the Civil War. He was a dashing man, experienced with women, eligible, successful, socially secure. His affectation of British mannerisms drew some of Glasgow's fretful ire when, years later, she characterized him as an eager climber. Anderson was a Republican, not the right party in Richmond, where a gentleman was expected to be a Democrat like his father.[22] Critical of the Democrat Woodrow Wilson, Anderson had some political aspirations and worked to improve Republican prestige in Virginia. In 1921 he won the nomination as the Republican gubernatorial candidate, but his campaigning was desultory.

Glasgow met Anderson in 1916 and they became engaged on July 19, 1917. She was forty-three. They exchanged many letters, full of emotion —hopes, anxieties, torments. He called her Vardah, an astrological nickname. There were intimate suppers at 1 West Main. But World War I significantly interrupted their love. As a colonel in the Red Cross, Anderson went to Rumania to direct the Commission to the Balkans. He became closely attendant upon the Rumanian Queen Marie, a granddaughter of Queen Victoria who was known for her beauty and magnetism. Anderson seems to have become personally entranced with her beyond the call of Red Cross duty. A year later he returned to Richmond. After spending the evening of July 3, 1918, with her fiancé, Glasgow took a nearly fatal dose of sleeping pills. Despite the deterioration of the engagement, Glasgow describes their relationship as one that continued, not always happily, for twenty years. Anderson never married and was attentive with gifts and visits. He finally appeared, unwelcomed by Anne Virginia, at Glasgow's funeral. Together with Glasgow's brother, Anderson sought to establish her house as a memorial landmark, but their efforts did not succeed. The house is today the Richmond Humanities Center used by the public schools.

As a public figure Anderson provided the model for several of Glasgow's characters: the political idealist David Blackburn in *The Builders* (1919) and Gideon Vetch, the "white trash" governor of Virginia who dies by an assassin's bullet in *One Man in His Time* (1922). Glasgow's impassioned disappointment over Anderson caused her to create numerous women characters who learn to live without love or happiness. It also accounts for her many heroines who feel they cannot breathe freely until they have survived their lovers or watched them die in miserable circumstances. Even then, their alleged relief is unconvincing. Gossip had it that Glasgow was "wild about Henry Anderson," had bought her trousseau, and hoped to marry him. After her death Anderson was extremely reticent about their relationship. But he said more than once that he thought her "very emotional . . . too much so" and that the two of them were perhaps too "individualistic" to marry. His conviction that "women are happier where the dominance of the man in the relationship is recognized, at least to the extent of his obligations,"[23] is interesting in view of Glasgow's own tendency in her fiction to exalt the strength of women and minimize that of her men.

Whatever the reasons for Glasgow's not marrying Anderson, theirs was a complicated relationship, both rich and wounding. Among her papers in a folder marked "miscellaneous pungencies" is found the following assertion of independence:

I have had a[s] much love and more romance than most women, and I have not had to storke [stroke] some man the right way to win my bread or the wrong way to win my freedom.[24]

Glasgow's domestic life settled into a routine with Anne Virginia Bennett. Although Miss Bennett had small literary appreciation of her employer's work, the two women had a *modus vivendi* that worked for over thirty years, until Glasgow's death. Among their interests in common, both women were devoted to animals. From childhood, Glasgow had made their welfare her abiding concern. She pitied "the larger unredeemed part of creation . . . the heathen . . . and . . . our lesser brethren the animals."[25] Favored characters in her novels are compassionate toward dumb creatures. Hunts and hunting imagery pervade her writing, always signifying cruelty and degradation. In Spain she refused to see a bullfight. She disliked jesting about the scientific value of experimenting with living animals and judged others by their attitudes on the subject. She became angry with her old friend, Walter Hines Page, for an article he wrote criticizing antivivisectionists. Though she found Theodore Roosevelt charming when she met him on a homeward voyage from Europe in 1914, she considered his African game hunting a barbaric exercise. Active in the Richmond Society for the Prevention of Cruelty to Animals. Glasgow served as first vice-president from 1911, then president in 1924. She raised money for the organization and made it an effective and prestigious outfit. In her will she endowed the society generously.

Glasgow's own pets were beloved companions. Perhaps, as a friend suggested, her deafness made it easier to communicate with them than with people.

Two dogs were notable—a pedigreed Sealyham, Jeremy, that Henry Anderson gave her for Christmas in 1921, and a French poodle named Billy. Glasgow and Miss Bennett would cavort with them in the garden. The dogs had expert medical attention from surgeons, not veterinarians. Their portraits were engraved on Christmas cards. In England Glasgow had collars and clothing made for them. When she traveled she included messages to them in her letters home.

When Jeremy died, Glasgow dreamed more than once of searching for him throughout space. In a poem, "To My Dog," she wrote that she would feel a traitor in prizing a heaven that did not admit animals. Jeremy and Billy received burial in the garden of 1 West Main Street, although her other dogs were interred in a special plot in the Pet Memorial Park of Richmond. Before Glasgow's death she gave instructions that the caskets of Jeremy and Billy were to be exhumed and placed within her own coffin. Her collection of ceramic dogs, many of them antiques of rarity and value, went to the Valentine Museum in Richmond. Always affectionately whimsical, Cabell wrote of Glasgow and her animals:

Now, in chief, does Ellen Glasgow love dogs; and second only to dogs, all forms of animal life except human beings; and thirdly, humane letters.[26]

Glasgow's was undoubtedly a strong and complex personality subject to contradictory moods. She might at times be cheerfully extroverted; she could be aloof and sardonic. She was a lavish hostess in the grand style to those whom she felt merited her attention. Some found her a well-read, intellectual conversationalist. Yet she could show a "pathological" invidiousness, according to Cabell, at the successes of other writers. Often she was wretchedly lonely, hungering for approval from an apparently indifferent world.

People wrote or spoke of Glasgow in varying ways. There was the cozy Ellen who would sit by the fire or in bed after her morning bath and breakfast, laughing and talking about family matters with her niece Josephine. Or she could be heard shrieking gales of mirth in an upstairs bedroom with her sisters and woman friends. Henry Anderson said, "She loved to laugh. She was witty," though in later years her humor turned to cynicism. Hugh Walpole wrote to her:

Dearest Ellen . . . I feel so close to you sometimes when I'm thousand[s] of miles away, I can hear you laugh. . . . People love what they call your maliciousness. Do go on being malicious.

Small, with "an almost doll-like round face," she had "a smile that was actually radiant, for her eyes brightened ineffably when she smiled." Anderson and other men pronounced her not at all beautiful, but her eyes were lovely. Counting on literary women to be dowdy, one observer found her surprisingly "always beautifully turned out." She would appear at one of her parties rouged, bronze-haired, brightly dressed in vibrant blue and little high-heeled blue slippers—for she liked color and adornment—in an elegant room fragrant with a cedar log fire and potpourri of roses.[27]

She surrounded herself with pleasant luxuries in her great grey stone house. There were the good eighteenth-century furniture and the flattering portrait of herself over the fireplace by the society painter Prince Troubetzkoy. From the vine-hung back piazza sitting room where she spent her mornings, she could enjoy the walled garden, with its evergreens and myrtles, mimosa, flowerbeds of petunias, and box. This garden, with its birdbath, was the prototype of the romantic garden in *The Sheltered Life* (1932). In the front of the house a magnolia grew, pink geraniums filled stone urns, and wisteria wreathed the iron fence. Glasgow wanted to be served, never to have to brew her own cup of tea. For driving, the liveried black chauffeur stood at attention with a blanket over his arm when he opened the door of the big Packard limousine for Miss Glasgow.[28]

Together with her taste for living well went a pleasure in sumptuous entertaining "with all proper pomps and fanfaronades." Glasgow received relatives, children, friends, old Civil War soldiers, and the literary world. She presided and talked, monopolizing the conversation, since her deafness made two-way exchanges difficult. "She would have dinner parties for 6 or 8 and talk—the dinner would drag on—," said Henry Anderson.[29] Her eloquence, however, was admirable. "She knew more about books than any woman I have known," wrote a visitor. "Her memory was phenomenal and she quoted poetry and even prose passages which she recollected without making any effort to tax her mind."[30] Several guests thought her talk far wittier than her novels.

Eventually, Glasgow obtained a hearing aid, a little black box that she carried with her:

She put her hearing aid in a little silver mug like a child's mug at the table. . . . She had to keep one hand to her ear to hold the other end of the attachment in place and she just pecked at her food with the other hand. She ate like a hummingbird. Her hands were like a child's hand. So tiny.[31]

With her hearing box, "she listened to one person at a time . . . ; she never heard the casual conversation of groups," wrote Julian Meade, who found it "remarkable that Miss Glasgow was so fine a novelist when she could never listen normally to the ordinary talk of people around her." The experience of having

Glasgow thrust the little mug at one in expectation of a swift reply to her witticism was said to be unnerving.

Glasgow cleverness and vivacity could edge into sharpness. Her precisely enunciated, aristocratic voice grew metallic. She would beam out her brilliant smile while saying "things that were as disturbing as they were true." Her "shrewishness," wrote Cabell, in discussing her successful contemporaries was "a never-failing well-spring of diverting malice"; her remarks about Willa Cather were as unforgettable as they were unrepeatable. She could be kind enough to young authors as long as they did not show signs of becoming too well thought of. She was not generally sympathetic with what "most young men in the South were trying to do" in their writing, and in her autobiography she disparaged expatriate authors, "all the bold young men, from the Middle West."[32] In fact Glasgow was outspoken in her sweeping scorn of contemporary letters, which she termed "obscene, amateurish, pompous illiteracy escaped from some Freudian cage." Privately, Cabell thought that her own writing "and the applause of her writing were the sole matters which concerned Ellen Glasgow vitally." Guests at the literary gatherings were expected to write pleasing articles. " 'All that I ask', she used to remark impartially, 'is admiration.' " When praise was not as loud as she liked, she grew bitter and attributed the lack of appreciation of her work to a general decline in taste. Cabell thought her "a lonely and baffled woman" who was unhappy the last twenty years of her life.[33]

Glasgow felt she had successfully hidden her wounded spirit from the world: "I was able to build a wall of deceptive gaiety around me," she wrote in *The Woman Within.* Her retreat was her room. "I

wanted a room of my own, and it was granted me,"
she declared; alone she confronted her unhappiness
and took refuge in work. In her room the family
could hear her pacing and declaiming poetry aloud
to herself so that they feared the servants would
think her mad. In her bedroom she would waken in
the night to "a drumming along the nerves to the
brain . . . in an upward march from the quivering
muscles of my body" and fall prey to "the ghost of
some old unhappiness."[34] It was also in a room of her
own that she wrote, and she finally felt that her work
was compensation, in fact the only life she had, for
her "burden of melancholy".

Glasgow's years were filled with trips to doc-
tors. She sought the help of aurists for her hearing,
psychoanalysts for her depressions. Toward the end
it was her heart that failed her. A severe coronary
attack in December, 1939, forced her at sixty-six to
the status of a semi-invalid. Other attacks were to
follow. For the six years of life that remained she
had to be careful, writing only in allotted periods,
sparing her strength. Nonetheless she insisted on
carrying on with her work and with the arduous
drives to Maine.

Eighteen days before her death, Cabell wrote to
Marjorie Kinnan Rawlings:

Two days ago I saw Ellen Glasgow, and her condition horrified me. She is a mere wisp and has reached really an
advanced stage of melancholia. She has been able to do
virtually no work for some two years, and she now faces
with horror the notion of living inactively in her dark
house throughout the winter with not even any literary
contacts. . . . She talks morbidly about being starved mentally as well as physically.

Urging Rawlings to write to Glasgow, Cabell suggests:

Tell her how wonderful she is in comparison with all other writers, living and dead; that is treatment to which she responds purringly.[35]

While Glasgow was getting a permanent wave in the Jefferson Hotel's beauty salon on November 11, 1945, she had another heart attack. Anne Virginia sent home for Scotch and administered half a glass. The permanent was hastily finished. Ten days later on the morning of November 21, 1945, Anne Virginia found her in bed; she had died several hours before, a serene smile on her lips.

A High Church Episcopal service was held on the twenty-third of November at 1 West Main. The house was massed with flowers. Ellen Glasgow was buried in Hollywood Cemetery in Richmond. The inscription on her tombstone was from Milton's *Lycidas;* "To-morrow to fresh woods and pastures new." In her will, signed on April 15, 1944, with codicils added the next year, Glasgow arranged for bequests to her sister and her niece, her friends and her servants. Anne Virginia Bennett, who had been with the Glasgow household for nearly thirty-four years, was left with an income for the rest of her life. On her death, the remainder of Glasgow's estate went in trust to the Richmond Society for the Prevention of Cruelty to Animals.

2

○○○○○○○○○○○○○○○○○○○○○○○○○○○○○

The Artist in New York:
The Descendant (1897),
Phases of an Inferior Planet (1898),
The Wheel of Life (1906)

Three early novels belong to Glasgow's apprentice-ship period, the years in which she was wrestling with her identity as an emerging writer. They are set in New York, which meant for the author and her characters an escape to intellectual Bohemia. By setting her southern heroines in this rich and alien milieu, Glasgow worked out her conflicting attitudes about her talent, her work, and her desire for love.

Each novel contains a woman artist torn between love and a whole-hearted commitment to her work. In *The Descendant,* the heroine is Rachel Gavin, a painter. The heroine of *Phases of an Inferior Planet* is Mariana Musin, a doomed singer who yearns for operatic roles but who knows that she lacks the voice. In *The Wheel of Life,* the main character is a poet in crisis, Laura Wilde. An adversary lover, husband, or fiancé, a man of demonic sexual and mental energy, fatefully appeals to each heroine. The heroes' stories are given as well, but the novels' authenticity lies in the plight of the women. In none of the three novels is there a lasting union. Failure or death undercut both love and art. Abandoned, Rachel survives a searing love affair to triumph as a painter while her lover dies. Mariana leaves her husband to become a music-hall performer, and she dies. Laura parts harshly from her fiancé, faces a breakdown, and renounces writing.

31

If the women characters exemplify the irrecon-
cilability of love and art, the male characters reflect
Glasgow's early reading program, for all are
freighted with political or social ideologies. They also
represent sexual temptation, together with a composite of attitudes that hinder each woman in her
single dedication to her work.

The Descendant (1897)

In *The Descendant*, illegitimate Michael Akershem
leaves his southern village and comes to New York.
After seven years he is the editor of *The Iconoclast*.
Cynical, despising humanity, he nevertheless falls in
love with the young painter, Rachel Gavin.

In her artist's garb and her rough yachting cap,
Rachel is an independent New Woman, "strange" to
the men eyeing her in the bohemian café they frequent. Her look is disdainful, her eyes deep set, inky-
shadowed, all brooding passion and challenge. Her
rich dark hair, slipping from her cap, foreshadows
her capacity for sensual abandon when she and Michael become lovers. Although Rachel came to New
York with introductory letters to her Southern social-
ite relatives in the city, she throws them into the fire.
Her preferred friends are street people.

Rachel works on an immense canvas of Mary
Magdalene, a subject of peculiar importance to her,
for the saint was a "scapegoat for the sins of men."[1]
The painting looks crude but shows the artist's talent
and understanding of women's suffering. Rachel will
require fuller experience to perfect her art.

Her conflict between work and love receives
close attention. A woman neighbor, a failed artist,
urges her to marry: "Women do. . . . You will too."
The idea horrifies Rachel. A seductive "devil" tor-

ments her, urging her to love. Her "angel" exhorts her to achievement, though the ascent is steep and barren. The struggle sickens Rachel. Men, it is assumed, can have both love and work. For a woman, love must extinguish intellectual and artistic effort:

"It is not fair!" cried Rachel passionately. . . . "Why should men have everything in this world?"

But she cannot resist Michael. The unfinished canvas is pushed away, and the lovers embrace in its veiled looming shadow. Now she is lost in a love "worth resigning heaven for, and worth walking barefoot to hell to gain." As a fallen woman, however, she can go nowhere.

While Rachel slips downward, Michael flourishes. Love soothes his old angry restlessness. His dazzling speeches make him seem the sane reformer. Leaving Rachel behind, he moves easily among the principal worlds of the novel: Rachel's studio; the men's world of newspaper office and club, where visionary schemes are constructed for the reform of society; and the dinners of socialites. The fashionable society that excludes Rachel eagerly lionizes him.

Under its influence, Michael grows conventional. He decides that Rachel cannot be a "good" woman and pursues instead a virginal young teacher whose social connections are acceptable. What he wants now are "the proprieties of life." Rachel "had given him life when he was famished, . . . passionately content to cast her art and ambition as a stepping stone, and on top of that her heart." Michael is weary of her sacrifice.

But when he thinks Rachel may have another lover, his vanity is wounded. At the same time, he begins to waiver in his loyalty to *The Iconoclast* and to angle for a more prestigious editorship. Taunted by a radical colleague for his defection to the paper, Michael feels uncontrollable rage. Abruptly he shoots and kills the man. He is convicted and imprisoned.

Michael's decline is paralleled by Rachel's slow regeneration. Weary and abandoned, she at first accepts hack work. Gradually she returns to her painting, finally completing the massive Magdalene. Her experience bestows a refinement and depth to her work. It is acclaimed at an academy exhibition and will be presented to the Metropolitan Museum.

After seven years, Michael is released from prison; broken in health and apparently tubercular. A vagrant, he finds his way to Rachel's studio. There he coughs blood, dying, while she silently exults, "He is mine—mine for all time."

The Descendant reveals Glasgow's early affinity with other writers of the naturalist movement in America. Literary naturalism occurred in phases and took various directions.[2] But authors under its influence shared the assumption that the novel could represent human life with scientific objectivity. Both physically and psychologically, human beings were seen to be part of the natural order and subject to its laws. Individual destinies, apart from the will, appeared to be materialistically determined by physics and biology, by heredity, by technology, or by social and economic necessity. Men and women might be depicted as aggregates of atoms, as organisms, animals, insects, or amoeba. When the hero of The Descendant reaches the city, he senses that:

Here . . . he was but one atom moving in its given line amidst many thousands. Then the denseness of population oppressed him, humanity jammed into a writhing mass, like maggots in a cheese.

As the helpless victims of impersonal forces, the lives of characters portrayed naturalistically are a struggle, their fates a matter beyond their individual wills.

For both lovers life is a struggle. Each battens on the other, and as one rises, the other falls. With Rachel it is her woman's biological nature, or "devil," that hampers her ability to proceed with her chosen life's work. As a Southern aristocrat, however, Rachel's innate toughness enables her painfully to climb toward regeneration, perhaps to triumph as an artist. She is a survivor.

Michael's life is traced in specifically Darwinian terms. An aspect of Darwin's thought was that human nature would develop through a combination of egotism and altruism. On the one hand there was the egotistic struggle for existence, on the other, the altruistic social sense, the basis of moral behavior. The irresponsibility that the illegitimate Michael has inherited from his parents is the innate flaw that will finally destroy him. Despite his efforts at self-improvement, the cultivation of his genius, and his taming through a woman's love, Michael basically lacks the social impulse. He fails in the capacity for altruism and generosity. He treats women selfishly. In committing murder, he reverts atavistically to brutal behavior. Michael is doomed when the element that emerges in him is

the old savage type, beaten out by civilization and yet recurring here and there in the history of the race, to wage the old savage war against society.

Originally Glasgow mailed the manuscript of *The Descendant* to the president of Macmillan, hoping for a decision within a week. A friend's brother who worked for the company agreed to lunch with Glasgow to discuss the book, which he had not read. Urbanely he plied her with wine and compliments and told her "to stop writing, and go back to the South and have some babies."[3] The manuscript, judged naive and pretentious, was rejected.

Glasgow persisted. She secured a reading from Harper's, where the novel's learned and naturalist tendencies led one of the editors to suppose it the work of a man. Harper's published *The Descendant* anonymously; the book created a stir and received a mixed reception. Hamlin Garland, the midwestern writer, pointed out the book's "grave faults" but gave it a generous review. He praised its "intellectual imagination," calling it "one of the most remarkable first books produced within the last ten years." The author, he wrote:

loves the clash of opinion, the war of creeds, the drama of the intolerant. . . . Her diction . . . is already distinctive, individual, and powerful, but with further study it will become still more flexible and exact. . . . She is a soul of deep earnestness, a writer not disposed to dodge, or pander to weak readers—a woman with something to say, and the will and the skill to say it well.[4]

But Glasgow's learning is obtrusive in this talky novel. She strenuously models her characters on ideas. Michael especially is a composite of revolutionary posturings. The novel's real interest shifts to the character of Rachel, whose dilemma is more convincing, just as it was more urgent to Glasgow. A minor work, *The Descendant* spells out with youthful pedantry issues that continued to occupy her: the subjection of humanity to social and physical forces, the battle between the selfish and the altruistic; the emerging of genetic strengths and weaknesses; and above all, woman's struggle for survival and autonomy.

Phases of an Inferior Planet (1898)

Encouraged by reviewers, Glasgow came out the following year with a second New York novel. *Phases of an Inferior Planet* is built of similar materials: the artistic bohemian girl from the South; her lover, a possessed, hard-driven intellectual; their doomed love. Mariana and Anthony marry. After the heart-rending death of their infant, Mariana leaves her husband to become a music-hall singer. In this novel, it is the woman who dies and the man who survives to devote himself altruistically, joylessly, to a life of social service.

"Phase First," which occupies two-thirds of the work, documents Mariana Musin's lonely hopes and the rise and fall of the marriage. Although New York means art and culture, the heroine shrinks from the smell of the ethnic crowd. Mariana is fortified by dreams of singing the roles of Elsa or Isolde.[5] Full of romantic illusions, she is content to live with her upright piano and her Japanese screen in a brownstone rooming hotel. The Gotham, at Ninth Avenue and Thirtieth Street, has a cast of regulars, grotesques who converge to feed meagerly in the basement dining room and engage in intellectual gossip.

Upstairs there are other aspiring Southern girls. These young women gather to mend their tattered underclothing and cook up messes of caramel candy, while chatting about men—the tyrants and tempters —and the life of art. They find it hard to concentrate on their work. One, a hopeful writer, confesses she hasn't written anything since coming to New York. The painting student is distracted by the availability of attractive men in the city. It is a revealing scene of young women unused to discipline trying to keep their lives and laundry sorted out, living in a shambles of pillows, guitars, "crude and fanciful and feminine" sketches, easels, caramels, palettes, half-used paint tubes, and Webster's unabridged dictionary serving as a footstool. When asked, "How do you ever find anything?" one girl poignantly responds, "We don't. We don't find, we just lose."

Here on a comic level the plight of Mariana is foreshadowed. The tone of the early scenes is lightly satirical, and there is some hint that Glasgow planned to deal ironically with her emotional heroine, who in fact lacks the requisite talent to fulfill her professional hopes. After the opening scenes, however, the novel abandons the comic mode and moves toward seriousness and pathos. Mariana realistically appraises her voice—it is good but not great. She marries an intense young scholar, Anthony Algarcife, whose monkish fervor contrasts with the unfocused enthusiasm of her girlish neighbors. Their married discomfort is realized to perfection. Mariana must learn to stifle her prattling and humming, the creaking of her rocker, and above all, her music. Secretly, Anthony thinks of art as "one of the trivialities of life." As Mariana abandons her singing, he rejoices in his influence.

Encouraged by her music teacher, however, Mariana considers a career on the musical stage. Her teacher urges her to remember "that you are an artist first, and a wife and mother afterwards, and you will succeed." But Anthony will not allow her to work.

Mariana becomes pregnant and gives birth to a tiny, sickly girl, pointedly named Isolde. When the child dies, a crushed, guilt-stricken Mariana feels "a canker within her heart": It is the thought that if she had been permitted to accept a singing position on the stage they might have afforded the child better care. The marriage has destroyed the husband and the wife. The turmoil of their passion has used up their energies and has been paid for by Mariana's abandoned musical career and Anthony's unwritten book. They part, Mariana to go abroad with a musical

company, Anthony to consider suicide, then to become an Anglican priest, Father Algarcife.

"Phase Second" opens after eight years have
passed. The pair is divorced. Mariana returns to New
York. She is rich, "fairer, older, graver," but her voice
is gone. Sadly she acknowledges, "I had the artistic
temperament without the art." There are attempts
to become reconciled with Anthony, but Mariana's
courage falters. Imagining that she will be wresting
Father Algarcife from a life of important service, she
feels that she has no right to claim him. What can she
offer? Only love. Sickened, she wanders through
rainy streets, finally dragging herself to her own
doorstep. She dies in Algarcife's arms. The disconsolate Algarcife once again considers suicide. But with
a fatal drug in his hand he is interrupted by a messenger bringing news of a strike. Algarcife goes forth
into the street to take up the challenge of social service.

In "Phase First," Glasgow nearly succeeds in
writing a self-contained novella. The sexual "life
force" that goads Mariana and Anthony into an incompatible marriage is sufficient to alter the course
of their lives, destroying their chances for significant
achievement. The woman pays the higher price because of her biological nature; nature's cruelty is a
fact that Anthony also acknowledges:

A physical disgust for the naked facts of life attacked him
like nausea. The struggle for existence, the propagation of
the species, the interminable circle of birth, marriage and
death, appeared to him in revolting bestiality.

Their child's death symbolizes, as it reveals to the
husband and wife, the end of the marriage. The domestic crises are convincing. The heavy display of
scientific erudition, as well as the flights into social
comedy with the humorous types at the Gotham,

tray an uncertainty of focus and detract from the stronger marriage episodes, however.

"Phase Second" is filled with contrived incidents, chance meetings, and jejune scenes of manners in the homes of the socialites who are Algarcife's parishioners. Algarcife's bookish, overwrought personality, apparently modelled on Glasgow's suicidal brother-in-law, Walter McCormack, lacks substance. The novel's abrupt ending is a flaw to be found, unfortunately, even in Glasgow's better novels.

Inept though it is, the novel raises the question, important to the author, of how much a woman should give up to become an artist if she has only the love of art and not the genius. What if she gives all to love and it doesn't work? What if she then gives all to her art and that doesn't work? Can she go back to love? Miraculously, in the novel, love seems still to be waiting. But by now the woman has spent her strength, her confidence. It is too late. There is a current of despondence: "I was never good enough," reflects Mariana brokenly: "I have always done wrong, even when I most wanted to be good." There is nothing left for her but to die, a punishment for having failed both in her womanly and her artist's role.

The Wheel of Life (1906)

After the critical failure of *Phases of an Inferior Planet*, Glasgow turned to her native region and published three novels about Virginia between 1900 and 1904.[6] When she returned to the theme of the anxious woman artist in New York, it was with a difference. In *The Wheel of Life*, the characters are pointedly caught up in literature. Far from seedy Chelsea and the cafés of Bohemia, the novel's conflicts are played out in comfortable brownstones on the East side of Manhattan. The heroine, Laura Wilde, lives in Gramercy Park with her eccentric Southern relatives in a house that has a ghostly, even Gothic aura. It has been in the family for years. The neighborhood, the deserted streets, Laura herself buried away in the "grave old house mantled in brown creepers," seem to a visitor to be "all creations of some gossamer and dream-like quality of mind."

Of the three apprenticeship novels, *The Wheel of Life* specifically explores the relation of literature to love. Is the fullness of erotic experience necessary to the writer's sensibility, or is it an obstacle? Shall the writer love? Shall she marry? If so, what kind of man? Laura Wilde, the poet-heroine, is loved by three men. Each of them would represent a different decision on her part. The sensual Arnold Kemper is energetic in his pursuit of "life." Roger Adams is a withdrawn and saintly type. St. George Trent, an aspiring playwright who also is infatuated with her, is too young for Laura to take seriously. But he represents the allure of literary success.

At the time of writing this novel, Glasgow had just lost her lover; the man she called "Gerald B—" in her autobiography had died. She sought consolation in reading philosophers and eastern mystics. In her dejection she found it hard to work. She turned to write *The Wheel of Life*, of which she explained afterwards:

I was seeking what I did not find, an antidote to experience, a way out of myself. I was trying to break the tight inner coil of my own misery. Emotionally drained, I had nothing to give. Yet I needed to live, and more even than I needed to live, I needed an escape into a world that could bear thinking about."[7]

Torn among the demands of love and sex, the desire for mystical withdrawal, and her belief in herself as a writer, Glasgow explores these concerns in *The Wheel of Life.*

Laura Wilde is at a turning point in her growth, since she wonders if her cloistered existence is keeping her from achieving excellence in her poetry. She longs for experience: "I want to taste everything." When the worldly, cynical Arnold Kemper pursues her, she is prepared to be shaken from her former resolution to remain "pure and apart."

Despite their mutual attraction, Laura and Kemper are so different as to be incompatible. He lacks her inwardness. He asserts, "I never think. . . . I live." He prefers cars to books, since they are bigger and faster. As for poetry—"Well, I take my poetry where I find it, . . . mostly in life and not in books." This attitude intrigues Laura. Art and life, so defined, seem to exclude each other. She gives up writing and agrees to marry Kemper.

But there are implicit warnings against matrimony in the examples of the two other married couples, Laura's closest friends. There are Perry and Gerty Bridewell. Robust Perry, captivated by any feminine ankle or pair of hips he observes in the street, is consistently unfaithful. His look, like Kemper's, is sexually vital, slightly brutal. Gerty, a beauty, is completely involved in the passional life. She is a slave to her body, with continuing anxieties about wrinkles, diet, and clothing. Marriage, she declares, is not "contentment" but "a battle—all the time—every instant. It isn't worth it, but I'm bound to it—I can't get away. I'm bound to the wheel."

The other wretched couple is Connie and Roger Adams. Here it is the wife who is unfaithful. Connie is unstable, shallow, baby-faced. Subject to hysterical depressions, she relies on the stimulation of affairs and cocaine. Her gaunt, long-suffering husband has the temperament of a mystic. When Connie dies during an operation, Roger reveals his austere love for Laura. Laura feels his moral superiority.

Despite these premonitions of the inauspiciousness of marriage, Laura becomes engaged to Kemper. He has no romantic illusions, feeling convinced that in a few years his excitement with Laura will have faded and that he will be bored as he usually is by women. But the engagement is ruptured by several incidents involving a former mistress of Kemper's, a plumed, scented soprano named Madame Alta. In a room heaped high with wedding gifts, Laura voices her deepest misgivings. Kemper, turning to leave, stumbles on a red leather box containing a silver coffee service, the burdensome paraphernalia of matrimony that threatens to impede him as well as Laura.

Laura takes a nocturnal ferry-boat flight from the city. There have been hints about her "wild," "trapped" nature. Her "instinct for flight is like that of a wild thing in a jungle." She is "a beautiful wild bird, helplessly beating its wings in the fowler's net." Her thirst is for a freedom that cannot be had in love, it seems. Since her work has failed her, she sinks into despair. After a healing period of withdrawal in the Adirondacks, Laura returns to New York, vowing to devote herself to charitable works. Perhaps the "secret of happiness, after all, might lie for her, not in the gratification but in the relinquishment of desire."

In Glasgow's third novel about the woman artist, the literary theme is pervasive. Adams is editor of *The International Review.* Even Kemper once wrote a shockingly male novel "with very little grammar and a great deal of audacity." St. George Trent is a playwright intoxicated with the thoughts of applause and footlights. For Trent Laura's personality is inti-

mately bound up with the glamor of her poetic genius. There is a starving young neighbor of Trent's,
Christina Coles, who carries about her parcel of
manuscripts "like a lioness defending her threatened
young." Trent and Christina are a potential literary
couple, but Trent's comical mother cannot approve
of lady novelists who expect to be taken seriously:

It's as if they really pretended to know as much as a man.
When they publish books I suppose they expect men to
read them and that in itself is a kind of conceit.

Except for Trent's successful play, these literary
notions and ventures come to nothing. Laura's own
loss of stability, her unnerved sacrifice of her art,
betoken a loss of faith in the word, written or spoken.
When we consider *The Wheel of Life* as a novel that
Glasgow admittedly wrote in a period of crisis, it is
not surprising that it should close with a statement on
the inadequacy of words:

There are moments charged with so deep a meaning that
all explanations, all promises, all self-reproaches become
only such vain and barren things as words.

This is the last of Glasgow's increasingly bleak
novels on the artist and her craft. Despite its pessimism, *The Wheel of Life* is superior to the others.
The author's learning, her reading in mysticism, are
incorporated more subtly. The writing is controlled,
even distinguished. As for the theme of the woman
artist, Glasgow evidently felt that the problem of
life and art had been worked out, for she did not
again recreate such a figure. The failure of love between all the couples of the novel would again surface as a theme central to her work after 1913, with
Virginia. Noteworthy for its deft, brittle scenes of
social comedy, *The Wheel of Life* contains the
repartee of parlor and boudoir that anticipates Glas-

gow's excellent novels of manners of the 1920s. Maxwell Geismar praised the work's treatment of "the illusion of desire, the disenchantment of possession," and thought it "probably the best work of her early period."[8]

3

○○○○○○○○○○○○○○○○○○○○○○○○○○○○○○

The Civil War and Its Aftermath:
The Battle-Ground (1902),
The Deliverance (1904)

The years in New York gave Glasgow a needed per-
spective on her writer's role and provided her with
the scene for the early works. In that same period she
was also thinking of a series on Southern life. Virginia
was home; there she had her most intimate, most
realistic sense of place. There her finest work would
eventually be rooted. She viewed her intention to
concentrate on the South as "a change of literary
base with me" and hoped, as she wrote her editor in
1899, to embark upon a group of books about Virginia.[1]

Writing about the Civil War was a way of summing up an entire epoch of Virginia culture and its
passing. Hundreds of novels have been written on
the war,[2] but Glasgow's *The Battle-Ground*, immensely popular in its time, stands as one of the
earliest attempts at a realistic appraisal of the conflict
and its implications for the future of the South.

The Battle-Ground (1902)

Glasgow's efforts at verisimilitude led her to research
the files of Richmond newspapers for the war years,
1860 to 1865, and to visit old battle sites. She based
some information on stories her parents had used to
tell. But her chief focus is on the manners, attitudes,

and illusions of the planter families, rather than on any of the solid realities of their lives. She saw those who fought as extravagant idealists:

men who embraced a cause as fervently as they would embrace a woman; men in whom the love of an abstract principle became, not a religion, but a romantic passion.

Her avowed purpose was to expose the lie of that romance, not only as it had obsessed and deceived those men and women who lived through the war and watched their illusions fade, but also as it was perpetuated by nineteenth-century writers of Southern fiction. It is obvious, however, that Glasgow at the same time viewed that romantic lie with an affectionate tolerance.

The Battle-Ground seeks to explain the old planter aristocracy and what it stood for, its manner of life before accepting defeat, and the spoliation of that kind of life. Dan Montjoy goes to war. The South is defeated and he returns, ill and ruined, to marry Betty Ambler, the strong girl who has waited for him. Together they will build a new life. The war's survivors finally are able to bid farewell to what they had defended: the privileged, graciously mannered life; the patriarchal order; the slave society; the excessive reverence for tradition; the hot defense of gentlemanly honor; the cult of the lady. These survivors would adapt to a new, unstable future with courage and patience. "I have tried," explained Glasgow, "to portray the last stand in Virginia of the aristocratic tradition."[3]

Events are seen through the experiences of two upper-class families in the Shenandoah Valley, the Amblers of Uplands plantation and the Lightfoots of Chericoke. Their family names—attributes of different kinds of horses—imply their fidelity to a Southern chivalric order soon to be outmoded. Both families are headed by men who represent the con-

trasting types of statesman and soldier, Governor
Ambler and Major Lightfoot.

Peyton Ambler, former state governor, has the
views of an enlightened intellectual. A slaveowner,
he is not at ease with the idea of slavery. His gentle,
toil-worn wife is altogether attuned to her duties as
plantation mistress. Their daughters are the docile,
lovely Virginia, and the independent Betty, the heroine.

Their neighbor is old Major Lightfoot, whose re-
miniscences go back to the battlefields of the Mexi-
can War and the War of 1812. For him fighting will
solve everything. His choleric martial temperament
makes him a foil to the more rational, thoughtful
unionist, Governor Ambler. The Major and his wife
have grieved quietly ever since their daughter
eloped years before with a hot-blooded scapegrace
named Jack Montjoy. The issue of that hasty union,
young Dan, is now orphaned. At sixteen, Dan comes
begging his way back to ancestral Chericoke, where
he is joyously welcomed.

Dan and Betty fall in love. The first two books of
the novel, "Golden Years" and "Young Blood," capture their romance and the innocent idyll of antebellum Virginia. Pleasures are family centered. Blacks
are portrayed as happy and humorous, with names
like Congo and Petunia. The Major and the Governor, just verging upon caricatures, exchange gentlemanly views on gout and slavery. While the Governor muses and hesitates on the rightness of the
institution, considering the proposal to allow the government to send the Negroes back to Africa, the pur-
pling Major thunders indignantly:

Why, you are striking at the very foundation of our society!
Without slavery, where is our aristocracy, sir?

The entire picture is of a mythical "old South" that
never was, in a romance that gently mocks itself.

Private and political events bring this period of innocence to a close. Rakish Dan, now nicknamed "Beau" Montjoy, quarrels with the Major over a college escapade. He leaves his grandfather's roof—repeating his mother's flight— for the Merry Oaks Tavern where he becomes a stage driver. His loyal black servant, Big Abel, follows.

The political events that disrupt society are the raid against Harper's Ferry, with its attendant fear of a slave uprising, and Virginia's eventual secession from the Union.[4] Lighthearted boys go forth to war, planning to be back home for the holidays.

The novel's third and fourth books, "The School of War" and "The Return of the Vanquished," deal with the war's major events. Dan's adventures take him from the first Battle of Bull Run, a Southern victory under General Beauregard, fought at Manassas Junction on July 21, 1861, to the news of Lee's surrender to the North on April 9, 1865. The bloodiest fighting, the cruelest devastation of the war, occured, it should be noted, in Virginia.

Dan Montjoy joins the infantry, with faithful Big Abel to look after him. Foppish soldiers preen and play at war, waited on by their servants. Montjoy has heroic notions culled from books, and specifically he reflects on an old engraving:

He saw the prancing horses, the dramatic gestures of the generals with flowing hair, the blur of waving flags and naked swords. It was like a page torn from the eternal Romance; a page upon which he and his comrades should play heroic parts.

His illusions are paralleled by Betty's, who, at home, turns the pages of a medieval tale of King Arthur in praise of love, war, and honor.

Dan soon faces war's realities, gradually at first with dusty marches and galled feet, then all too soon in the turmoil of battle. He is sickened at the sight of men mangled like rabbits. Yet at times he feels himself seized by a primitive battle frenzy that strips away the veneer of civilization. Throughout the four years of the war, Dan grows up, passing through the hardening experiences of ragged fatigue, hunger, wounds, and sickness. His loss of illusions enables Dan to free himself from the burden of the past laid upon him by the family legacy—the aristocratic Lightfoot arrogance and irresponsibility, the Montjoy "bad blood."

Relationships are explored among the different white classes of fighting men. Dan forms a close comradeship with Pinetop, a gigantic mountaineer who, though not a slaveowner, will defend Virginia soil:

At the call to arms he had come, with long strides, down from his bare little cabin in the Blue Ridge, bringing with him a flintlock musket, a corncob pipe, and a stockingful of Virginia tobacco.

When Dan finds Pinetop studying his primer by a winter fire, he is shocked to realize that Pinetop is a victim of the system that keeps down the poor white. Dan helps Pinetop learn to read and prepares himself for the idea that these two classes—poor white and planter—must soon join forces to work together for a new South. Humorous Pinetop is a folk hero, an appealing if somewhat idealized representative of the poor white, whose plight Glasgow would develop in other novels.

Glasgow also deals with women's hardships. Betty does heavy farm and house chores and waits for Dan. Her pregnant sister, the weaker Virginia, stumbles through a makeshift hospital to look for her wounded husband. The heat and the sights of raw wounds tended by surgeons with reddened hands prove too much for her. At home her wild thoughts

mingle with the scent of the fiercely blooming magnolia in the garden. She miscarries and dies.

When Dan learns of the South's defeat, he
weeps. He takes out his jackknife, cuts up the Confederate flag, and gives each of his comrades a fragment, keeping one for himself. Having lost his old
glorious vision of flags waving, he performs a gesture
symbolic of the future, sharing of anguish and responsibility among the South's survivors.

Dan returns home broken in health. He is filled
with a sense of the war's waste. The old past is gone.
Chericoke has been burned to the ground. Strong
Betty greets Dan with maternal solicitude; together
they will face an uncertain future, making a living
from the soil.

Instead of regretting the past, Glasgow's Southerners cast doubts upon that fleeting world. The
older and the younger generations react in their separate ways. When Governor Ambler gets the first
news of the slave uprising, he suffers a crisis of conscience. In their revolt he sees a "savage justice," for
the slaves are attempting to overturn a social order
that was founded upon a violation of natural laws. He
views the coming war as a heavy payment laid upon
his and future generations for wrongs committed by
their forebears. Yet he will die fighting in an effort to
quell the murderous powers that have been un-
leashed.

For the younger generation, on whom the
weight of the future will fall, the past will be easier
to dismiss. Dan will not die of his wounds or of his
wounded spirit. His stamina shows him to be one of
Glasgow's Darwinian heroes, able to survive and
adapt to a radically changed environment. Dan's
final reflections on the old carefree life are less intel-
lectualized than the Governor's. To him it is "like the
dim memories from some old romance."

The obliteration of the past is viewed positively. The hardships of war and peace liberate Dan from the fate he might have had in continuing the pleasant traditions of Chericoke—that of a corpulent, self-satisfied planter. Now he is more manly, less selfish, more respectful of other human beings. He has learned the necessity of sharing the future with others and laboring for a strong South.

Glasgow tends, however, to omit the blacks from this utopian scheme, even though she considered their enslavement to be a transgression of natural law. She would continue to portray them as more or less contented to serve. Dan cheerily accepts Big Abel's offer to labor for him:

"Let yo' darky do a bit of work if he wants to," [Abel] urged, "but it makes me downright sick to see one of General Lee's soldiers driving my plough."

Instead, in Glasgow's fictional vision, the rising South is largely the affair of the whites. The novel offers several examples of poor whites, not all so charming as Pinetop. The South's future would be a contest and collaboration between them and the decayed planters.

The two contrasting female characters, the submissive, doomed Virginia and the survivor Betty, a little wiser and stronger than her man, are important types that recur, with variations, in the later fiction.

The Battle-Ground whimsically creates a storybook picture of the Old South and systematically sets out to dismantle this picture. It attempts to destroy the romance of war and expose its furies. The characters, however, remain fixed at the level of caricature or of endearing exemplary types. There is no effort to develop an adult relationship between the lovers Betty and Dan, who conduct themselves with ingenuous propriety. Good blacks are loyal and workaday,

electing to remain in their servile status even after
they have been freed. The well-behaved poor white,
Pinetop, is sentimentalized in his ignorance and pa-
triotic fervor. With its essentially innocent vision and
hints of social comedy, *The Battle-Ground* remains
one of Glasgow's minor successes that might appear
intended for juvenile readers.

The Deliverance. A Romance of the Virginia Tobacco Fields (1904)

The time is from 1878 to 1890. It is twelve years since
the close of *The Battle-Ground*. After the South's
defeat in the Civil War, the region has made painful
efforts to reestablish its depleted economy. Planter
families who have lost everything are laboring to
wrest a living from the soil, just as the survivors of
The Battle-Ground had determined to do.

For every type of farmer tobacco is king. There
are descriptions of its growing in "rows of bright-
green leaves that hung limply on their slender
stalks," with swaying blossoms rising tall and pink.
Workers pinch off the suckers. The leaves are cured
with open fires in clay-daubed log pens, scenting the
air of the whole countryside:

From the roof the tobacco hung in a fantastic decoration,
shading from dull green to deep bronze, and appearing,
when viewed from the ground below, to resemble a num-
berless array of small furled flags.

Tobacco is favored over corn, "a lanky, slipshod
kind of crop." There is a wealth of homely lore about
its virtues. Infants can nurse and teethe on a plug of
tobacco. A girl will wear a sprig in her leghorn hat.
"It's better to water yo' mouth with tobaccy than to
burn it up with sperets." Dark leaves make a sweeter

chew. A cigar is gentlemanly. "The man that ain't
partial to the weed can't sleep sound even in the
churchyard."

Glasgow's interest in the crop and landscape of
her native Virginia was more than picturesque. The
local topography became a metaphor for her art and
its inspiration. The life of the region was "a fertile, an
almost virgin field," which could "yield a rich harvest" to a novelist. Its surface had been merely
scratched by earlier writers:

The soil was deep and dark with a thick deposit of unused
material. . . . I felt that farther down there was a vital
warmth, the warmth of humble lives that have been lived
near the earth.[5]

The Deliverance deals with those lives at three social
levels. There are the members of the now decaying
aristocracy who had to resort to small farming to
survive, the former poor whites who had profited
from the war and were farming big estates, and the
simplest of rustics who hoed at their patches of
ground and hung about the village store to gossip.

The novel's two chief families, the aristocratic
Blakes and the humble Fletchers, have exchanged
places as a result of the war. The Blakes, once rich
planters, have lost their slaves and ancestral home of
two centuries; they live in the overseer's cottage.
The ill-mannered, upstart Fletchers, the family of
the former overseer, have prospered and now own
Blake Hall.

Each member of the Blake family is affected dif-
ferently by misfortune. Christopher Blake is a giant
of the soil, splendid in appearance but barely literate.
When the war was lost, he had to plough instead of
study and he now supports the family. His twin, Lila,
adapts herself by showing her willingness to marry a
yeoman farmer. Old Mrs. Blake, frail and august in

lace cap and black brocade, sits blinded and par-
alyzed in her Elizabethan chair, never having been
allowed to know of the South's defeat. She represents
"the lost illusions of the Southern heart."[6] Her older
daughter, Cynthia, once a belle, is a worn-down spinster of forty. She labors with roughened hands to
maintain her mother's comforts, at the same time
feeding Mrs. Blake's delusions that they are still living in Blake Hall and that Virginia has permanently
seceded from the Union. Cynthia's pleasure in life is
the "luxury of lying." She is a verbal artist, spinning
a web of fiction about the dead past, much like those
nostalgic authors of the antebellum romances.

Christopher longs for vengeance against
Fletcher, the poor white who bettered his fortunes
since Reconstruction[7] and fraudulently acquired
Blake Hall. Christopher feigns friendship for
Fletcher's grandson, Will, and corrupts him. He
goads him to drinking, hunting, and marrying a slat-
ternly poor white girl. Fletcher reduces Will's inheritance, and Will waits to wreak his own vengeance on
his grandfather.

The third group of characters are the poor local
farmers who gather in the tobacco barn or the general store to comment on the doings of their betters
and to provide exposition. Among these are Susan
Spade, the storekeeper's wife, one of the first of Glasgow's sharp-tongued, angular women who deliver
choice apothegms on human frailty. She is cynical on
the subject of "natur,' " which she regards as "a tick-
lish thing to handle without gloves." Usually she
comments with asperity on the relations between
the sexes: "Well, trouble may be born of a woman,
but it generally manages to take the shape of a man."
Indeed, much of the conversation of all these characters tends toward cynical observation on romance
and marriage.

While Christopher plots against the Fletchers, he falls in love with Fletcher's granddaughter, Maria. He had once rescued her from his pack of dogs in the fields and inadvertently flicked her face with his whip, an incident revealing his contradictory passions. Beautiful Maria, educated and matured by an unhappy marriage and widowhood, has developed a conscience. When she learns how her grandfather acquired Blake Hall and that the mansion has been willed to her, she determines to restore it to Christopher, its rightful owner.

Maria's brother, the now degraded Will, finds that she and not he is to inherit Blake Hall. He drunkenly attacks old Fletcher with a hammer and kills him. Christopher's recognition of how well his vengeance has succeeded sobers him at last. He claims guilt for the murder, stands trial for Will, and goes to prison. He serves three years, when Maria secures his pardon and release. Will confesses the crime. Maria's love delivers Christopher from his past, his ignorance, his raging hatred, his demons. The deaths of old Fletcher and Mrs. Blake also deliver the young from the evils of the old order.

Three forces shape the characters' lives in *The Deliverance*. These forces, operating in conjunction with one another, are history, environment, and heredity, both biological and cultural.

History, in the form of the Civil War, had already done its work in reversing fortunes and social positions. But history is an ongoing process that continues to change families and individuals long after the war's end. It was Glasgow's purpose "to interpret ... the prolonged effects of the social transition upon ordinary lives."[8] The war has entombed Mrs. Blake in a living death. It has driven Cynthia to urge her brother to vengeance. Christopher is said to be "the embodiment of a period in violent transition; and in

this transition the dark tumult of war had been cast
up from the torn earth and had entered the open
mind of a child."[9] Thus, the violence of history
becomes translated into the lengthy conflict and tormented action of the novel's main character.

Environment is more than setting. Not only does
the earth provide a livelihood, but it affords an identity for all who live close to it. Cynthia in the midst
of her toil yearns to lie in the field "to renew the vital
forces within her by contact with the invigorating
earth—to feel Nature at friendly touch with her lips
and hands." Her compulsion to labor prevents her
from indulging this desire.

Especially does Christopher, once the son of a
great landowner and now a ploughman, reveal a kinship with his environment. Glasgow wanted to "construct a scene in which the human figures would
appear as natural projections of the landscape."[10]
Christopher appears "as much the product of the soil
upon which he stood as did the great white chestnut
growing beside the road." In his movements "there
was something of the large freedom of the elements." Maria sees him with hair fair as wheat, skin
like terra cotta. As his rage for vengeance begins to
dominate him, however, he ceases to be identified
with the earth and its vegetation and degenerates
metaphorically to an animal.

Christopher's growing animality becomes evident as he grapples with his demons and devils. He
smells of the stable. He prefers to eat with his dogs.
He is called a "hell-hound." He wants to satisfy his
"hatred until it should lie quiet like a gorged beast."
"Fate had driven him like a whipped hound to the
kennel, but he could still snarl back his defiance."
The hunt is a subtheme. As a beast, Christopher
becomes both prey and a predator. He teaches Will
to hunt. He flees like a hunted animal from the mem-

ory of Maria. The scene in which he saves her from his dogs is later paralleled in a dream in which he has set his hounds on a hare. The mangled hare turns into Maria, who asks beseechingly why he hunts her to the death. The final purging of the beast within him results from his expiatory prison term, where, sick and wasted, he has lain with other "animals," that is, his fellow criminals.

In contrast to the repressed Cynthia and the degraded Christopher, the widowed Maria returns from abroad to reaffirm her bond with the land. She discovers her deep and abiding care for the simple, wild country of her origins. However enchanting the foreign places she has seen, what Maria loves are "the desolate red roads, the luxuriant tobacco fields, the primitive and ignorant people." Her romantic identity with the region is an indication of her growing sensitivity, her capacity for love, and the redeeming power she will be able to exert over Christopher.

Heredity is the novel's third operative force. This is understood in two senses, the biological and the cultural. First, there are the physical and mental traits that are transmitted to offspring by their progenitors. These qualities Glasgow terms "blood." Second, there are the cultural traditions that individuals may inherit from their ancestors, but which may also be acquired—through books and education —by other members of a society.

Glasgow's interest in "blood" or "race" leads her to speculate on the inborn characteristics that the ancestral Blakes have bequeathed to Christopher to make him what he is. When Christopher leaps to stop a runaway horse, inadvertently saving young Will from death, his uncle Tucker Corbin tells him: "It's in your blood to dare everything whenever a chance offers, as it was in your father's before you." But he is also subject to the Blake disease of apathy—"that

hereditary instinct to let the single throw decide the
issue, so characteristic of the reckless Blakes." They
had been selfish, careless:

Big, blithe, mettlesome, they passed before him in a long,
comely line, flushed with the pleasant follies which had
helped to sap the courage in their descendants' veins.

As a result, Christopher appears to be "a fine racial
type" mingled with "sheer brutality." He is "a pure
fleshly copy of the antique idea." The "high-bred
lines of his profile stood out clear and fine as those of
an ivory carving." But he has a "coarsened jaw."

Christopher's inherited qualities, both bad and
good, might have been corrected and refined by education if he had had the opportunity to follow his
inclination for learning. But the cultural inheritance
was denied him when postwar events kept him from
going to school. It is therefore for Maria to come to
his aid, to redeem him through the learning which
those same events enabled her to acquire.

Maria, despite the vulgarity of her father, has
inherited her mother's superior genes. She is strong
enough to be a savior of the fallen Blakes. Her womanly qualities include ardor: rather than gentility; she
is capable of a show of spirit toward any misogynist
who would "air camphor-scented views of [her] sex."
Her vitality and generosity make hollow the aristocratic pretensions of the older Blake women. Born
into the poor-white class, then, Maria is able to rise
to the level of a lady through education.

A sign of Maria's development into a person of
worth is the separate library she has created for
herself at Blake Hall. She has gathered books, not
the kind most women read, Glasgow notes, but the
works of philosophers, French novelists, and classical poets. Some of Glasgow's ambivalence emerges,
for she hastens to add that feminine touches, such

as scattered pillows, relieve the scholarly scene. By acquiring the "heritage" of the leisured aristocracy Maria can return this legacy to Christopher, from whom it was torn. Among the books she reads aloud to him is the medieval *Quest of the Holy Grail.*[11] The lines she reads celebrate the renewal of spring and love, as well as the ability of lovers to "call again to mind old gentleness and old service and many kind deeds that were forgotten by negligence." Intoxicated by her words, Christopher feels that her effect on him is to divide him "like a drawn sword from his brutal past." Maria redirects him to his lost traditions.

The Deliverance was extremely popular in its time, both with the public and with reviewers. It sold over a hundred thousand copies in the first year of its publication. Readers admired its insider's view of tobacco farming as well as its naturalism, the powerful effects of environment and circumstances upon character. Glasgow's Virginia scene, that of tobacco-growing yokels and dispossessed planters harrowed by passions born of the war, was a departure from the nostalgic literature of the period. A pioneering achievement, the novel anticipates the more masterly novels of William Faulkner, with their bitter tensions between poor whites and decayed aristocrats.

While Glasgow had carefully analyzed the forces she believed would determine character and hence destiny, she was not content to pursue the unrelenting consequences of these forces. She was a naturalist only up to a point. She thus strains the reader's credulity with the character of Christopher Blake, whom warring forces have reduced to a helpless level of bestial rage. Instead of allowing him to deteriorate altogether, she sentimentally saves him. After hatred and vengeance have poisoned his thoughts for nine years, his conversion to love under Maria's tutelary influence is hardly convincing.

Glasgow was trying to formulate a blueprint for a better social order, proposing the idea that superior strains of white heredity could be salvaged, mated, and propitiously blended with aristocratic values. Vital Maria and a regenerate Christopher, inspired by the ideals of the Holy Grail, regain the ancestral Blake mansion. It was characteristic of Glasgow to seek solutions that would embrace both past and future, but the preferred culture is the aristocratic legacy of the past. Humbly born Maria has to become a lady to earn her way back to Blake Hall. Her superior woman's strength, her education, and her independence are to be directed to the saving of the degraded Southern aristocracy, notably the weakened man she chooses to love.

The novel's shortcomings lie in its sentimental treatment of the two principal characters, whereas minor humorous figures succeed in their unvarnished homeliness. *The Deliverance* also excells in its vigorous sense of design and imagery, its evocation of place, its brooding interpenetration of past and present.

4

○○○○○○○○○○○○○○○○○○○○○○○○○○○○○○○○

Political Men of Virginia:
The Voice of the People (1900),
The Builders (1919),
One Man in His Time (1922)

Glasgow's Virginia pride inspired her at various times to document aspects of the state's political history. The oldest commonwealth in the South and in America, colonial Virginia was rich, populous, aristocratic, and steeped in English traditions. Early in America's history, native Virginians became distinguished statesmen and leaders to the nation, from Washington, Jefferson, and Madison to the Confederate General Robert E. Lee, who had been a colonel in the United States Army. With the Civil War, Virginia's political and military prominence declined. In writing of the South's recovery after the war, Glasgow recognized the need for Virginia to generate leaders once again. The political man of vision and action occurs in three novels. How far could he go, however determined, however gifted? What were the chances of the poor man in Virginia, where clannishness, class snobbery, and reverence for tradition were so strong? Other issues in the novels are the provincialism of the region that had led Jefferson to speak of Virginia, not America, as "my country," the rival interests of the farmer and the aristocratic politician, the entrenched racial attitudes, and the solid loyalty to the Democratic party machine.[1]

Glasgow's first Virginia novel, *The Voice of the People*, traces the rise and fall of a farmer's son who becomes governor. It is one of the earliest fictional treatments of the poor white to avoid ridiculing him as a type. Toward the end of World War I, Glasgow returned to the political novel with *The Builders*. Its hero, a patrician of impoverished childhood, desires Virginia to serve the nation on the verge of war. Her third and last political novel was written after World War I. The hero of *One Man in His Time*, viewed askance by members of the proud upper classes, is a circus-bred poor white who becomes Virginia's governor. In each work the political man is an outsider and his fate is infelicitous. Both poor-white governors are assassinated, while the upper-class hero has to accept personal unhappiness and an uncertain political future.

The Voice of the People (1900)

With the departure of Reconstruction governments from the South after 1869, native Southerners had the chance to control their own state governments. Politicians emerged from two groups: the upper- and middle-class Bourbons comprised former planters, lawyers, and businessmen, while the agrarians were farmers and men of humbler station. Both political groups appear in *The Voice of the People*, but the farmer-hero transcends his class interests and tries to represent all constituencies honorably.

Nonetheless, the "clash of class," a favored theme of Glasgow's, is evident. It is also a conflict between the ways of the present and the past. The present was immanent in the lives of the new men of the poor-white and small-farmer class who were pushing their way into prominence, wealth, and social service, places formerly preempted by the aristocrats. The aristocrats aligned themselves with the past, with patriarchal culture, the cohesiveness of clan, and family honor. These aspects of the traditional code function in the romantic plot.

The past also resides in a civilization's historic monuments, both architectural and intellectual—its landmarks, its buildings, its books, and the words of its writers. Wanting a setting with the aura of old Virginia, Glasgow visited Williamsburg, which was the capital in colonial times. The old courthouse and its green, the College of William and Mary, chartered in 1693, and its library, are monuments that figure importantly in *The Voice of the People*.

The novel covers the years from 1870 to 1898 in Kingsborough, representing Williamsburg. The hero is carrot-headed, square-jawed Nicholas Burr, son of an overworked peanut farmer. He becomes Virginia's governor. He then campaigns for the Senate. Shortly before the election he tries to stop a lynching mob. Unrecognized, Burr is shot and killed.

The chief Kingsborough families are the struggling poor-white Burrs, benevolent Judge Bassett and his son Tom, the embittered Civil-War widow Jane Dudley Webb and her son Dudley, and the proud Battles of Battle Hall, consisting of the old General, his son Bernard, his daughter Eugenia, and two maiden aunts. On the outskirts of the town are the negro hovels to which the former slaves have come back after Emancipation.

Nick Burr's family is caught in the futile daily round of work. His stepmother, Marthy, is a trenchant commentator on woman's lot, a country type at whose portrayal Glasgow excels: "T'ain't the water buckets as bends a woman, nohow; it's the things as the Lord lays on extry." Her dissatisfaction with the government as well as with the Lord accurately reflects the feeling of farmers and their wives that conservative politicians ignored their plight:

"It's the lawful wives as have the work to do, an' the law-fuller the wives the lawfuller the work. If this here government ain't got nothin' better to do than to drive poor women till they drop I reckon we'd as well stop payin' taxes to keep it goin'."

Marthy is sympathetic to Nick's desire to study. Along with a few well-born boys, Nick gets lessons from Judge Bassett.

But Dudley Webb's mother objects to her son's being taught with an inferior like Nick, who is "common as dirt." Jane Webb is a confirmed mourner for the Confederacy:

At her throat she wore a button that had been cut from a gray coat, and, once, after the close of the war, she had pointed to it before a Federal officer, and had said: "Sir, the women of the South have never surrendered!"

She is the archetypal South in defeat, rigid and uncompromising. "Her pride was never lowered and her crepe was never laid aside."

Another upper-class family with whom Nick is involved are the Battles. Bernard is a ne'er-do-well. Eugenia and Nick fall in love, although her family disapproves. The neighboring blacks, too, think there should be no "intermixin' up er de quality en de trash."

Nick's family asks him to relinquish his study because they need his income. When he pleads with his father to let him continue to read with the Judge, tobacco-spitting Amos Burr's laconic reply is, "Thar ain't much cash in that, I reckon." Nick reads at night, working in a store by day. This occupation confirms his servile status in the eyes of the neighboring aristocrats.

Then Eugenia hears that Nick has made the storekeeper's daughter pregnant. Although Bernard has in fact seduced the girl, Eugenia prefers to break with Nick than to accept her brother's guilt. She re-

treats into the stronghold of her class and marries
Dudley Webb. Theirs is a joyless marriage, but Eugenia proves incapable of any action save loyalty to
the clan. The "Battle breeding" has emerged "more
invincible than the Battle virtue."

Nick throws his energies into his work, gets
through the University, and sets up a law practice in
Kingsborough. When he runs for governor he campaigns against his boyhood schoolmate, Webb. Webb
belongs to the old "race of patriots"; Burr is an idealist. Generously he refuses to discredit Webb for lob-
bying with bribes on behalf of a railroad company.
When Burr wins the election he determines to ap-
point "clean men" even if it means going against the
machine. He refuses to restrict suffrage, which would
effectively exclude blacks from the polls—although
the mere hint that a candidate would accept black
votes would have ruined him in the eyes of the white
supremacists.[2]

As governor, Burr performs an act that endears
him to the aristocrats. He secures a pardon for his old
enemy, Bernard Battle, who has been convicted of
forgery. Overcoming his hatred of the Battles means
more to Burr than all his political successes; he considers pardoning Bernard "the victory of his life."

When Burr is slain at Kingsborough, Webb goes
on to win the election. Burr's death leads his friends
to glorify his memory, but they reflect that he was too
good for them. Eugenia's thoughts turn from Nick's
heroism to the continuance of her class. For Eugenia,
motherhood of the race is the destiny she readily
accepts. The apparently happy Webb family group at
the close ironically points up the cohesion and invul-
nerability of a morally imperfect patrician class.

Burr looks superficially like an agrarian type. He
is plain-talking, unlike the Bourbon rhetoricians.
Farmers support him, since "the people think he has
the agricultural interests at heart." Willing to depart

from the party machine, he resembles the independent group known as the Populists,[3] an agrarian party seeking relief and reform for farmers. Only in Virginia did these independents succeed, though temporarily, in displacing the Bourbons from office. The movement failed just after the 1896 election, which would have been at the time of Burr's assassination.

Burr rarely grapples with issues, however. Above partisanship, he is meant to appeal both to rural and upper-class interests. The narrative locates him in place and time: He is both a product of the soil and a sharer in Virginia's historical and learned traditions. As a would-be agrarian, he is sentimentally identified with the Virginia countryside. He revels in morning ploughing. His changing fortunes are "fair weather" or "a rainy season." As a statesman whom the Bourbons would accept, Burr is pictured against monuments: old buildings, the college library, Capitol Square, Washington's statue, the bound volumes of the Codes of Virginia.

Somnolent Kingsborough, with its ancestral portraits, shuttered houses, and tranquil streets and gardens, is steeped in history. Its battlefields are grown over with grass, its Civil War veterans still gather in the general store to rehearse their wounds. The present museum was once a church, before that a powder magazine. Despite these changes, "Kingsborough was the same yesterday, today, and forever."

Burr studies in the Kings College Library, moved by the "words of great, long-gone Virginians":

He felt the breath of hushed oratory in the air, and the political passion stirred in the surrounding dust.

For him Virginia's great past lies in its monuments and in the divine principles of the ideal statesman,

Jefferson. It is the inheritance of which all Virginians can be proud.

But the old planter families, entrenched in class snobbery, care little for the great past. Bernard is corruptible, Webb full of rhetoric. Eugenia responds with bored distaste at the idea of enrolling in the Daughters of Duty, whose aim is to save Kingsborough's landmarks, so dear to Burr. Nor does she care for the legacy of Virginia's statesmen. Grown cynical as a politician's wife, she laughingly admits that

"The first lesson in politics is to lie and love it; the second lesson is to lie and live it. Oh, we've been to Congress, Dudley and I."

Burr's disillusion comes after he has been elected governor. As a boy he had wanted to "become learned in the law" like the Biblical prophets. Now he recognizes politics as trickery and juggling.

The law's failure is most evident in Burr's murder. He invokes the law before a vengeful lynching mob:

"Men, listen to me. In the name of the Law, I swear to you that justice shall be done—I swear."

They shunt him aside, while a contemptuous voice from the crowd shouts: "We ain't here to talk." Burr's reverence for Virginia soil, Kingsborough's monuments, Virginia's statesmen, the law itself, prove ineffectual. The law neither saves the hero nor enables him to serve a society barricaded in its complacency. While Burr is destroyed, the smug old ruling class lives on, seemingly invulnerable, intent on the continuance of its race.

Glasgow apparently seeks to warn and punish her own class by indicating that better men are on the rise from the ranks of the poor white. But if

picturing Burr against landscapes and monuments
statically conveys his attitudes, it fails to bring him to
life. All grim will and determination, an unap-
preciated underdog, he is merely a conflation of
ideas. Eugenia's characterization is itself also flawed
by the author's ambivalence, for Glasgow is caught
between a secret admiration for her and the need to
condemn her arrogance. As usual, however, Glasgow
offers realistic sketches of minor humble folk with
whom she had no ideological ax to grind. Noteworthy
too is her prophetic understanding of the subtle canker of racism and of the lawlessness it unleashes.
(Burr, politically friendly to blacks, accidentally dies
in a lynching incident.) The novel's other strengths
arise from its celebration of country life and its often
brilliant accounts of the Virginia social and rural
scene. A pioneering rather than a major novel, *The
Voice of the People* shows Glasgow in greater control
over setting than character.

The Builders (1919)

Glasgow's first political novel was set in a time within
memory of the American Civil War. Now, writing of
the outset of World War I, she makes her hero a
Virginian of good family that lost its money. David
Blackburn has been deprived of a gentleman's education. He has worked at factory jobs, studied inde-
pendently, and become a wealthy steel industrialist
in Richmond. He is, at forty, a man of fiery "eternal
principles," so much so that his supporters, northerners and southerners both, hope he may be elected to
the United States Senate. Here Glasgow moves away
from the local concerns of state politics and considers
what is the best Virginia can give to the nation on the
eve of an international war and a presidential election. The period is the autumn of 1916.[4]

Blackburn wants to build the nation with "great dreams," with religion and morality. He also aims to break the stranglehold of the Democratic party machine in the South, and then to urge southerners to put aside sectional sentiment to join other Americans in fighting the war. Whereas "the great Virginians of the past had been Virginians first, the great Virginians of the future would be Americans." By going to war together, the nation would emerge from a baptism of fire "clean, whole, and united."

Blackburn's political ideas arise from reported conversations, letters, and private harangues scattered throughout *The Builders.* He dislikes the Democrat Wilson's current campaign slogan pledging peace and prosperity, a promise he finds cowardly and "unctuous." He had voted Republican in 1912. His abandoning the party of his fathers arouses the disapproval of the old guard, who think there is something "black" in a man who votes Republican. But Blackburn also concedes that the Republicans may have difficulty in the South, since the memories are "too black."

Referring to the Republican administration during Reconstruction, when black men were granted the rights to vote and hold office, Blackburn reveals his racial views:[5]

"[T]he offices of local governments were filled either by alien white men or by negroes; and negro justices of the peace, negro legislators, and even negro members of Congress were elected.... [T]here are things worse than death, and one of these is to subject a free independent people to the rule of a servile race; to force women and children to seek protection from magistrates who had once been their slaves."

Still, he will not vote for the Democrats. Determined to vote not so much for a man as "against a section," Blackburn suggests that he may support Chief Justice

Charles Evans Hughes, the 1916 presidential candidate endorsed by the Republican and Progressive
parties.

Glasgow based Blackburn's ideas on those of her
friend and one-time fiancé, the lawyer Henry W. Anderson, who stated that he drafted speeches and
whole chapters.[6] Since Glasgow published *The
Builders* in her name without credit to Anderson,
she apparently found his views acceptable. Here as
in most of her novels she omits any meaningful social
or political consideration of the Southern black.

The romantic plot of *The Builders* is evidently
Glasgow's invention. A woman of thirty-two who has
had an unhappy love affair, Caroline Meade is a re-
builder—of her personal life. She takes a post as
nurse for the Blackburns' delicate little girl, Letty.
Letty's mother, Angelica Blackburn, is a beautiful
frail selfish creature, one of Glasgow's sickly sweet
ladies who destroy the happiness of those around
them.

Caroline quickly learns that Angelica neglects
her child. The servants, canny about their betters,
mutter darkly against her. She pretends her husband
mistreats her. She hampers his career wherever possible, for she thinks of politics as ill-bred. She under-
handedly incites a malcontented worker whom
Blackburn fired. She hints that her disreputable, alcoholic brother, Roane Fitzhugh, is being encouraged as a suitor of Caroline's in order to discredit her
with David.

Caroline comes to distrust Angelica, and to admire and love David. In him she sees "some vein of
iron that you can't break, you can't even bend." She
values him for his wish to transcend the parochial-
ism of the region, comparing him to "the men who
laid the foundation and planned the structure of
the American Republic." Unable to put his ideas

into practice at home, David goes to France to fight. Angelica's evil nature is fully revealed when she breaks up the engagement of her sister-in-law, Mary, for she hopes to win for herself Mary's wealthy fiancé, Alan Wythe, once she secures a divorce from David. Alan is killed in the war. Angelica, truly ill now, decides to stay with David and their child. David and Caroline love each other but renounce their happiness. Caroline will go to France as a nurse. Sacrifices have been made by so many in this war; a strong national future will require further unselfishness.

Caroline is the author's independent, responsible woman. Not given to brooding "among the romantic ruins of the past," she will spend her best energy in "service and pity." She can live without love. Glasgow shows that wars make sensible women even stronger. Caroline's determination reflects what is best in the Southern women looking to the future, whereas Angelica's feigned frailty masks a viciousness representing the evils of a privileged past.

The characters in *The Builders* are too stereotypically ranged within the camps of good and evil to be interesting, and it remains an inferior work. The universal admiration for Blackburn appears forced, for his speeches are filled with resoundingly empty rhetoric. *The Builders,* not a success with the public, was the only novel of Glasgow's to be serialized; it appeared in *The Woman's Home Companion* in October, November, and December of 1919.

One Man in His Time (1922)

This is the last of Glasgow's novels of political men, one in which she tried to frame a formula for the

ideal leader. Her hero is the circus-bred Gideon
Vetch. His socialist aims include nationalizing key
industries. Vetch is sure that once he has manipu-
lated the party machine to get into office, he can, as
"Independent" governor, achieve reforms to benefit
the people. But the people are an unstable entity and
would prefer to manage their governor. Vetch also
makes enemies among unscrupulous men who
helped elect him. During the strike that threatens for
much of the book, Vetch is killed by an assassin's
bullet.

The setting is post–World War I Richmond. Two
social groups are represented—the aristocratic old
guard and the rising poor whites. All are freighted
with histories and attitudes that render them types
rather than individuals. There is hope that the in-
teraction between the two white classes, sealed by a
marriage, will enable the South to renew itself. Un-
realistically left out are the blacks, who have no political or indeed any existence save that of a servant
caste who reveal their own prejudices by deferring
with insolence toward their employers, formerly
poor whites.

Ranged on the side of the patricians are the two
chief characters, young Stephen Culpeper, a World
War I veteran who has been nervously afflicted by his
military experiences, and his vibrant cousin Corinna
Page, who is in her late forties. Both are steeped in
tradition but are eager for wholesome change.

Stephen returns to Richmond morally unable to
reenter its sheltered world. He resists family pres-
sure to marry Margaret, a quaint girl who is chauf-
feured about in a hearselike automobile. His attitude
hardens against his family when he discovers the
source of their wealth. Generations of well-mannered Culpepers have thrived on high rents
squeezed from rundown tenements that are "the

Culpeper estates." Disillusioned by their hypocrisy and by the war, with its clichés about improving the world, Stephen feels that only a passionate love can heal his soul. Piquant Patty Vetch, the Governor's daughter, charms him against his will. She seems to be a new cause, "the red flower he dared not wear." The love between Stephen and Patty is scarcely motivated, and seems little more than an idea that tradition now and then needs a transfusion.

Corinna Page, presented as one of the last and best of the Southern great ladies, is of Glasgow's age and outlook. Corinna holds court in her old print shop surrounded by tapestries, bowls of roses and marigolds, and English mezzotints. With her autumnal beauty, she looks as if she had stepped from an old painting. A "flower of the Virginia aristocratic tradition," in her are gathered the ideals that her forebears had brought to these shores, fought for, and bequeathed to their descendents. She presides over her tea table and chats with her elderly gentleman callers before the cedar log fire. This is a scene for which Glasgow had a clear affection, even while she mildly mocks it. The well-bred, intellectually honest Corinna stands for romance, mystery, and authority. She clings to the beautiful things and elegant manners of the fading past even as she looks with wary hope to the bracing reformist politics of the new age.

The other representatives of Richmond's aristocracy are caricatures, with their high-nosed Roman features and their suave confidence in the divine right of their status. A general, a judge (Corinna's father), and a lawyer named John Benham, who is a conservative opponent of Vetch's, gather in Corinna's print shop to gossip about politics and society. Their views reveal them to be incapable of development.

Benham tranquilly woos Corinna. He has all the

advantages of birth, education, and manners. Despite his reputation as a statesman, he is unmasked as a hypocrite in his betrayal of Alice Rokeby, a vulnerable woman who has secured a divorce for his sake. Corinna sees him as a dry, thin-blooded, effete member of the aristocracy at its selfish worst. A rigid theorist in politics and in human relations, he is personally heartless, and he is a foil to the vigorous Vetch, whom he despises.

Gideon Vetch, principal among the lower-class characters, arouses varied reactions. Corinna recognizes his physical magnetism and muses about him as a possible lover. The invidious accuse the circus-bred governor of demagoguery. He charms the riffraff and is the people's tool. He admits making important political appointments as payoffs to his supporters. He does not look like a gentleman in his rumpled plumage, he smokes an inferior cigar and hesitates over the silverware. To his friends, however, he looks solid. His brow bulges intelligently. He radiates the warmth of the charismatic common man. He is his own best apologist:

"Now, I am a part of returning nature, of the inevitable rebound toward the spirit of liberalism. In the thought of the people who voted for me, I stand for the indestructible common sense of the American mind. I am one of the first signs of the new times."

Vetch's proposed reforms include pensions for the aged and for mothers, the government's control of mines and railroads, a decent wage, an eight-hour workday, jobs for veterans, proper housing for the black and white poor. Whereas his supporters consider him the people's savior, his detractors find his promises smack uncomfortably of socialism.

Glasgow tries hard to make Vetch look like the ideal politician, but both he and Benham, his opposing type, are doomed to fail. Vetch has "jolted us into movement," but he lacks "education, system, method." Benham, on the other hand, is "as logical as a problem in geometry." But he lacks adaptability and is deficient in humanity. The "leader of the future" should "be big enough to combine opposite elements; . . . he must vitalize tradition and discipline progress." Corinna adds that "He must accept both the past and the future." In the absence of the ideal, Vetch is better than Benham, for he has "human sympathy—the sympathy that means imagination and insight." But the violence of the times, which he has helped to nurture, does not permit him to live.

The political theme of *One Man in His Time* is a matter of theory. Livelier, and of greater moment to Glasgow, is the plight of her spokeswoman, Corinna, and her relationship with younger Patty Vetch. Corinna stands midway between her gracious traditions and the desire to be part of the present. Despite her "unspent fire of romance," Corinna determines to do without love. She accepts that hers is a "life like a deserted road filled with dead leaves." Glasgow implies that Corinna, like herself, is too strong, too finely regal for most men to appreciate, and that male preference is for shallow prettiness. "There ought to be something more permanent than love to live by," she thinks, like others of Glasgow's women. Her solution is to become a vicarious spouse to Vetch by mothering Patty, whose manners and style she sets about improving and whose energy stirs her. The tender womanly bond between Patty and Corinna arouses in her emotions that are like "those of first love without the troubled suspense."

Patty is a "Virginia redbird" who wears scarlet as her characteristic plumage. She has youthful buoyancy and charm but no facial bones and "no blood that one could mention in public." Her parentage

eventually turns out to be not Vetch but a criminal
mother and unknown father. Her greatest recom-
mendation is her unabashed admiration for Corinna
and gratitude for her queenly condescension. Patty's
metamorphosis is signaled by the emulation of her
patroness and a change of clothing: Corinna replaces
her flapperlike feathers with the garb of a medieval
page. Glasgow evidently struggles to like flighty
Patty, to find something positive about her abundant
energy. But in fact this energy is allowed no object
of its own. Instead, Patty, like a circus creature, appears willing to be harnessed by Corinna and Stephen to serve the needs of these wearied and disappointed patricians.

The ongoing contest in *One Man in His Time*
rages between the new times and the old. Will the
future bring beneficial change, or does it spell medi-
ocrity, a lack of values, chaos? Is anything worth saving from the past beyond the memory of great
achievements? Corinna cherishes the aesthetic, the
lingering loveliness of the Old South—the quaint
Georgian doorways and gardens, lavender-tinted
twilights, sunsets like apricots, "the ivy-grown corner
of an old brick wall; . . . the plaintive melody of a
negro market-man in the street."

The aesthetic is the ruling metaphor. The new
culture and politics are forms of pop art. The present
is a spectacle, a circus, a movie, and movies are responsible for introducing "the mock heroic into politics." Vetch is "theatrical" and a "mountebank" with
his "new circus blood." Upper-class styles of personal
beauty are compared to art objects and monuments.
Aristocratic-looking men resemble an Egyptian carving, Roman coins, an early American portrait. Culpeper is like the bronze statue of Washington.

Women's beauty is also seen in terms of high or
popular art. Corinna and Margaret look as if eight-

eenth-century artists had painted them. Corinna seemingly has stepped from a Romney portrait, although she supposes that the uncultivated Vetch, blind to her value, sees her only as a gilded picture frame. Alice Rokeby is a melancholy Byzantine saint. Red-gowned Patty, before her reclassification as a medieval or Renaissance image, was "like a picture on the cover of some cheap magazine," her charm "as well advertized as the newest illustrated weekly." A minor character is "as handsome as a Red-Cross poster." Cinema, circus, popular theater, poster and cover art herald the degradation of contemporary values. As in *The Voice of the People,* politics acquires an aesthetic dimension in which the artifacts or monuments of an earlier time project a humanism which the present lacks.

One Man in His Time shows Glasgow's growing preference for writing discursive fiction, making do with more talk and less plot and characterization. She groups her characters into pairs and trios according to sex, generation, philosophical outlook, class, or sensitivity. Generally they are type-cast, with the possible exception of Corinna, who serves as an idealized self-portrait of Glasgow in middle life.

5

○○○○○○○○○○○○○○○○○○○○○○○○○○○○○

The Growth of the New South:
The Ancient Law (1908),
The Romance of a Plain Man (1909),
The Miller of Old Church (1911)

Glasgow's Virginia novels were launched in 1900 with a political novel, *The Voice of the People.* Others explored the post-Reconstruction growth of Southern industry and commerce that rose up, as it were, out of the Virginia soil. In this period the Southern agrarian economy was giving way to manufacturing and business interests. "New South" was a term popularized by various journalists to encourage southerners to build mills, factories, and railroads, to develop scientific farming and public education, and to invest in commerce. Glasgow documents the transition as it affected the lives of individuals from the proud to the humble.

Members of the former landed aristocracy suffered social and moral traumas. Some of them tried to make the adjustment to a commercial or even a working way of life. Others lived on as parasites, unable to accept the reality of their changed status. Certain of this caste are judged severely in *The Ancient Law,* as well as in *The Romance of a Plain Man* and *The Miller of Old Church.* Many are disparaged as weak, selfish, even destructive. They cling to an old code of birth, family, patriarchal culture, and manners and to a superior sense of race and class. Adherence to the code does not ennoble them, however, but serves as a self-justification for hollow, often cor-

rupting pride. Significantly, the worst of these people
are capable of treating their own families with the
same inhumanity they extend to those lower on the
social scale.

The central figure of each novel is a virtuous
male protagonist who begins with a handicap,
whether of birth or error. He will seek to improve
himself while challenging the entrenched superiority of a still strong, still influential upper class. But the
old order stands fast, resisting him, and he must cir-
cumvent it as well as he can. This pattern informs the
plots of the three novels and is their ostensible subject. In fact, the heroes fail to engage us; the true
business of living is being carried out in the domestic
subplots, at the hearthsides, in the kitchens and
drawing rooms. Beyond its stated purpose, each
novel contains a richer underlife, largely of women
characters who express Glasgow's true concerns during the period of Southern change: suffrage, satire
upon marriage, the fundamental lack of understanding between the sexes, the bonding of women, and
feminine strength in adversity.

The Ancient Law (1908)

Middle-aged Daniel Ordway has emerged from a
five-year prison term for embezzlement. Like many
of the South's displaced aristocrats, he went to New
York after the Civil War to enter business. He specu-
lated on the stock exchange with others' money and
lost. Ordway still feels the stigma of his crime. As his
respectable family in Botetourt County do not want
him back, he leaves them to their prosperity and
begins anew in the simple community of Tap-
pahanock. There he will devote his life to altruistic

service, helping farmers, women, and a teenage alcoholic named Kit Berry.

Ordway moves easily between the two social groups of Tappahannock—the plain folk and the decaying aristocrats at Cedar Hill. Chief among the former are the unquenchable Mrs. Mag Twine, with whom he boards. Mag Twine's rage for soap and water impels her to scrub the hides off her awed children. Mag is one of Glasgow's gallery of spunky, strong, hardworking women, with an entertainingly sharp tongue and an endless gift of gab on menfolk and marriage. After two husbands, her passion for temperance has drawn her to marry a third, a drinking man. A weak woman, avers Mag, could not have taken on all three. When Bill Twine is carried off by "delicious tremens," the peace and quiet of widowhood get on her nerves and she marries a fourth husband. As Mrs. Buzzy she reflects upon the predictable habits of her current husband. "Naw, suh, it ain't the blows that wears a woman out, it's the mortal sameness." Of husbands generally, she observes: "So far as I can see one man differs from another only in the set of his breeches—for the best an' the worst of 'em are made of the same stuff, an' underneath thar skin they're all pure natur'." Her mistrust of human nature, or "natur'," is a mark of her Calvinist orientation.

Ordway also acts as friend and confidant to Harry Banks, an amiable lovesick youth. Banks sighs for pretty Milly Trend, the daughter of Tappahannock's mayor, Jasper Trend. Ordway becomes drawn into the political life of the town as well. Trend is losing his support as mayor, and popular Ordway thinks of running for the office.

When Ordway finds better lodgings with the fallen aristocrats of Cedar Hill, Beverly Brooke and his wife Miss Amelia, he joins members of his own class. The enervated Brookes have been sapped of any authority they may have possessed. Foolish, unpractical Mr. Brooke doesn't pay his debts. Miss Amelia seems "the disembodied spirit of one of the historic belles who had tripped up and down in trailing brocades and satin shoes." When their straits humiliatingly force the Brookes to rent Ordway a room, Mr. Brooke has firm notions on the difference between old-fashioned hospitality and how to treat a lodger:

"If he were an invited guest in the house, I should feel as you do that hot suppers are a necessity, but when a man pays for the meals he eats, we are no longer under an obligation to consider his preferences."

The Brookes' hardworking young kinswoman, Miss Emily, represents the best of the aristocracy: Her view of her life's purpose is to ease other people's burdens. Ordway and Emily are attracted to each other, but he has to tell her about his wife and family from whom he has separated.

Ordway's friendship with Emily and his political aspirations end abruptly when a stranger comes to town. This is slick Gus Wherry, an exconvict and bigamist. When Wherry courts the mayor's daughter, Ordway's conscience forces him to unmask the man, even though it means confessing his own prison past. He gives up politics and goes back to the family home.

At the mansion in Botetourt, Ordway finds himself a misfit. The family treat him with distant correctness. Especially does his wife Lydia make it clear that their married life is not to resume. One of Glasgow's coldly beautiful upper-class women, she retreats within her invalid's role, surrounded by satin hangings and bearskin rugs. Ordway's rebellious daughter Alice defies both her parents and elopes with a sensually attractive, socially inferior, wealthy man. The marriage is stormy. When Alice's spend-thrift habits impel her to forge a signature to pay for a fur coat, Ordway nobly steps forward and covers her crime by pretending he had promised her the money. Once and for all he leaves corrupt Botetourt.

Arriving at Christmas in Tappahannock, Ord-way finds changes. The older Brookes have died, leaving their tiny fortune to an orphan asylum while their own children are penniless. Emily will be forced to teach in a northern school. Banks and Milly have discovered the disillusionment of the married. Glasgow's difficulty with conclusions leads her to pile up events in almost random fashion. When a strike threatens the cotton mill, saviorlike Ordway uses his inheritance to buy it, so guaranteeing fair work con-ditions. But he is ill and burdened and decides to go west. On his journey he becomes delirious, imagining himself still in prison. The faithful Banks follows Ord-way to bring him back to Tappahannock. Ordway's final hope of helping the local people with their mills, schools, and libraries extends to a futurist vision of growing, thriving towns everywhere.

A minor work, *The Ancient Law* received little acclaim, popular or critical. Glasgow tended to clas-sify simplistically the worse and the better human beings of both the aristocratic and the humbler classes of society. The aristocrats have their evil strong, their evil weak, and their virtuous members. Those fittest to survive are readily tagged by the author. Ordway's entire family represents the heart-less, self-seeking, though flourishing relicts of the ar-istocracy, accustomed to having their way. The para-sitic Brookes, also selfish, are too weak to endure, though they are able to perpetrate harm upon their disinherited children. Sketched with a few humorous

strokes, the Brookes are not allowed to develop and
remain grotesque. Ordway and Emily are the only
exemplary characters of their class. Emily, disgusted
with "hereditary idleness" and dedicated to labor in
the service of others, is "the spirit of the future rising
amid the decaying sentiment of the past." Ordway,
unacceptable as a political leader because of his
prison record, contributes his class's inheritance of
wealth and idealism to the new world of Tappahannock. Unfortunately, Glasgow insists overmuch on
his virtues, and he emerges rather wooden. In the
unlikely events of the latter part of the novel, ailing
Ordway's accumulating of good deeds lacks conviction. A false note is struck, moreover, when he takes
offense at the imitation lace curtains in Tappahannock. Hoping to establish Ordway's gentility, the author succeeds only in making him a prig.

Among the poor of Tappahannock the same hi-
erarchy of types exists. Gus Wherry and Jasper Trend
represent coarse-grained, malignant commoners,
while poor, tearful Mrs. Berry and her spineless son
Kit are at the ineffectual bottom of the heap. The
upright folk include simple, good-hearted Harry
Banks and the quasi-moralist Mag Twine Buzzy.
Mag's views on the precariousness of the married
state afford a pertinent commentary on the novel's
disastrous or comic marriages. Mag Buzzy's scenes
are the most entertaining of the novel, and she is one
of Glasgow's genuinely delightful and unforced
achievements.

By relegating Mag to the peripheral status of a
minor choral character and bestowing her earnest
attentions upon stereotypes like Ordway and Emily,
Glasgow reveals herself unaware of the extent and
potential importance of her comic gifts. Her error in
The Ancient Law is to bloat and sentimentalize her
ideological characters. Those products of her imagi-

native genius, the low characters, seem to appear unplanned on the scene and remain unintegrated. Ordway never reacts humanly to Mag. After she says her lines, she is thrown away. Apart from Mag, and the occasional incipient comic characterization of the Brookes, *The Ancient Law* is a failure.

The Romance of a Plain Man (1909)

This was the first novel Glasgow set in the city of Richmond, later called Queenborough. It covers the period from 1875, just before the end of Reconstruction, through 1910. The city, recovering from the Civil War, was beginning to assume commercial and industrial importance. Society too was changing. The formerly landed families either subsisted in genteel poverty or adjusted by sharing in the city's commercial growth. New men of humble origins were coming to the fore.

The hero is the average "plain man," Ben Starr. He narrates his rags-to-riches rise: He marries an upper-class girl, makes, loses, and remakes fortunes, suffers a crisis in his marriage, and turns down the presidency of a railroad company to save the marriage. The novel also stages the social comedy of the old aristocrats who linger on with their outmoded values. Members of this caste will clash with the new men of action, like meteoric Starr, from whose enterprise the city actually stands to benefit.

Starr recalls his parents' frame house with its print of David attacking Goliath, a foreshadowing of his life's course. His mother, Susan, is another of Glasgow's plain women; she is anxious-eyed, hollow-templed, and clad in a gray wrapper and shawl. She is of that class who spend their days at washtubs, ironing boards, and funerals. Full of tart comment about

women's lives, she yet sinks down, overstrained and
overworked, and dies by her stove. When Ben's father brings home a new "female," Ben and his dog
decide it's time to go.

Ben glimpses the aristocratic world of "en-
chanted garden" Richmond in the person of little
Sally Mickleborough. Gravely she sizes him up as
"common." He labors to become worthy of her by
gaining wealth and importance. On his way to the
top, Ben finds an ally in the vigorous General Bolingbroke, who has made the successful shift from
Civil War leader to business tycoon. Among other
things, he is president of the Great South Midland
and Atlantic Railroad. As Bolingbroke's assistant,
Starr aspires to become his successor. Starr's vision
of bright tracks embracing Southern fields reflects
the region's optimism of the 1880s in the building
of the railroads.[1]

While he shyly courts Sally, her aunts, Miss Mitty
and Miss Matoaca Bland, receive Ben with reproach-
ful reluctance. In their view, worldly success, even
good character, cannot make up for social inferiority.
Sally's aunts represent "moth-eaten tradition," the
aristocracy at its most arrested point. They mildly
desire to move with the times but are capable only
of limited growth. These ladies guard the past as they
guard their ancient furniture. They entertain Ben
but abhor him.

Despite their opposition, Ben and Sally quietly
marry. Hardships befall the pair. Their infant son
dies. They suffer losses in a crisis that resembles the
Panic of 1893.[2] After a period of poverty and Ben's
sickness, he foolishly speculates with Sally's money
and loses again. Throughout, Sally is superb. She
comes through with characteristic upper-class fortitude, taking in fine lace to launder and making des-
serts to order.

By the time Ben makes his second fortune, the marriage has gone wrong. He has sunk himself too wholly in his work. In uncertain health, disconsolate Sally takes up hunting and riding with her cousin George at the family's country estate. When the long-coveted presidency of the railroad is offered to Ben, he turns it down. Instead, he will devote his life to Sally. They will take up their new lives in California, the marriage taking precedence over the husband's professional life. Both will turn their backs on the tyrannies of the Virginia family and the economic power structure.

Insofar as *The Romance of a Plain Man* deals with Starr's determined ascent into the ranks of the former aristocracy, most of the characters belong to that caste. They include those who can change with the times and those who, like Sally's aunts, cannot. The most adaptable are Sally and the General. The General has proved himself a survivor by entering business. In society with the ladies, however, he turns into a comic blusterer on the lines of Major Lightfoot in *The Battle-Ground* and Judge Battle in *The Voice of the People.*

When there are opportunities—and the novel offers many—to expatiate upon woman's place, the General, here a rigid caricature, takes up an antebellum Southern position on feminine sweetness and self-denial: "Marriage is full of sacrifice, and a man likes to feel he's marrying a woman who's fully capable of making it." These discussions usually occur in the Bland drawing rooms. As there is an old love story between the General and Matoaca, their conversation easily veers toward men, women, and marriage. The General in his rakish youth seduced another woman; Matoaca refused to marry him, maintaining that his obligation was to the woman he disgraced.

Matoaca, although entrapped in class prejudice where Starr is concerned, does, however, entertain the new feminist thinking. Considered "cracked," she timidly endorses women's emancipation and campaigns for suffrage. Glasgow plays comic variations for the first time on women's condition and rights.[3] The main characters voice opinions. Ben would be reluctant to have his wife go to the polls. The General exclaims to a male friend:

"What rights does a woman want, anyway, I'd like to know, except the right to a husband? They all ought to have husbands. . . . But rights! Pshaw! They'll get so presently they won't know how to bear their wrongs with dignity. And I tell you, Doctor, if there's a more edifying sight than a woman bearing her wrongs beautifully, I've never seen it."

In the Bland drawing room, he taxes Matoaca:

"But what would you do with a vote, my dear Miss Matoaca," he protested airily. "Put it into a pie? . . . A woman who can make your mince pies, dear lady, need not worry about her rights."

The refrain to this theme is taken up by the chorus of humble comic figures in the kitchens of Ben's mother and her friends. There, women's lives and rights, husbands, wife-beating, and motherhood provide continuing topics for shrewd discourse. After Mrs. Starr's death, maternal, curl-papered Mrs. Chitling takes care of Ben as a working lad. She holds forth in her kitchen kingdom: "What does a woman want with rights, I say, when she can enjoy all the virtues. What does she want to be standin' up for anyway as long as she can set?" Thirty years later, another kitchen crony, Mrs. Cudlip, quotes Ben's long-deceased mother. On women's submissiveness, she recalls, " 'The woman that waits on a man has got

a long wait ahead of her,' was what she used to say."
And on the matter of marriage generally:

" 'Thar ain't room for two in a marriage,' she used to say,
'one of 'em has got to git an' I'd rather 'twould be the
other.' "

Glasgow could with humorous cynicism venti-
late these views among her low characters. But her
mind appears divided on suffrage when she tells of
the fate of Matoaca, who literally dies for the cause.
Her last act is her march. Horrified, Ben sees her:

There she was, in her poke bonnet and her black silk man-
tle, walking primly at the straggling end of the procession,
among a crowd of hooting small boys and gaping negroes.
Her eyes, very wide and bright, like the eyes of one who
is mentally deranged, were fixed straight ahead.

Flushed, clutching a white flag, the "inspired spinster" collapses under the emotional strain and dies,
while the crowd howls. Matoaca's last gesture for
suffrage is made to look hysterically ineffectual. The
author's ambivalence forces her characters' various
voices on the subject to sound comic or pathetic.
Sally, a serious character, does conclude after years
of ups and downs in marriage that "poor Aunt
Matoaca was right":

"Right in believing that women must have larger lives—
that they mustn't be expected to feed always upon their
hearts. You tell them to let love fill their lives, and then
when the lives are swept bare and clean of everything else,
in place of love you leave mere vacancy."

Despite this ringing declaration, the novel leaves the
matter unresolved. For Sally, presumably, love is allowed to return to fill her life.

The Romance of A Plain Man shuttles between
the domestic scene and the world at large, each of
which impinges and reflects upon the other. Starr's

childhood, his aspirations, his love for his wife, and the continuing conversations about the relations between the sexes belong to the private realm. The public sector is concerned with questions of social change, the South's industrialization, the growth of the railroads, financial panic, the suffrage movement. Although she seems to be dealing with both private and public matters, Glasgow's real talent was for the former—the interior scenes, manners, and social comedy both high and low. The structures of power, industry, and money are too shadowy to explain the character of the hero.

Glasgow has difficulty in making Starr plausible —a business magnate single-mindedly bent on success who then gives up all for love. His self-absorption and romantic idealism seem more convincing than his drive for power, which the reader is asked to believe in rather than to observe at first hand. Interestingly, Glasgow transfers to Starr the problem that she as a novice writer had identified with the woman artist, that of the ultimate conflict between work and love and the necessity of choosing between them (see Chapter 2). She expressed her own dissatisfaction with the way she had handled the narration, feeling "that for a woman novelist it was a mistake to let Ben Starr tell his own story."[4] The preponderance of "feminine" interior and domestic scenes, as well as the pervasive discourse on snobbery, marriage, and the condition of women leave Ben far behind. Slow-witted Starr remains almost as entrapped in notions about woman's place as the General. Moodily caught up in his reveries, he becomes the opaque, rather childlike reflection of issues he never fully or finely appreciates.

Neither the public nor the critics were enthusiastic. Glasgow had reiterated her familiar themes— the contest between past and present, the plain people and the well born, women and men, the adaptable survivors and those unable to change. In the marriage of Ben and Sally, Glasgow tried to stress the importance, as she saw it, of pairing the best both classes had to offer. Sally, inherently strong and loving in adversity, declares, "I am my father's daughter, as well as my mother's . . . . I can bear anything and bear it with courage—gaity even." In Ben we have the homely vigor of the new man who will stand up to the forbidding members of Sally's class "as the living present of action stands to the dead past of history." Despite the novel's overall failure, it contains genial satire. The powers of the recalcitrant, corrupt, and frivolous members of society are amiably exorcised through Glasgow's comic vision. The humorous characters, especially the women of both classes, are well-wrought caricatures of their several positions. Typically unaware of where her strengths lay, Glasgow located at the center of her novel the stolid, cardboard Starr. The felt life of the work is at its periphery with the marginal female characters.

The Miller of Old Church (1911)

Here Glasgow unfolds her panorama of postbellum Virginia, showing the rise of new men in the country. The setting of this exuberant rural romance, the most self-assured of Glasgow's early works, is Southside Virginia at the turn of the century, between 1898 and 1902.

Three families of differing social levels find their fates variously bound up together, usually more than they wish. There are the aristocratic Gays, living at the great house at Jordan's Journey, the poor-white Merryweathers, one of them overseer to the Gay mansion, and the yeoman Revercombs, of whom

Abel Revercomb is the robust young miller of the title. One of Glasgow's honest plain people, a reader and a thinker, he is distinguished by his capacity for self-improvement. He shows promise of serving the entire society when he runs for the legislature (an offstage event).

The novel stresses the blood, stock, and racial characteristics of each family. The Gays are daring but irresponsible. The Merryweathers are dully submissive. The dark strain of illegitimacy links the Gays and the Merryweathers, their surnames a clue to their careless abandon. Certain of the Revercombs have the "vein of iron" in their genetic composition. Sarah Revercomb is an indomitable matriarch of sixty whose Calvinist background makes her suspicious of any kind of happiness. She is often treated with humor. Her gardening specialty is growing lilies for funerals. Her granddaughter is fair, voluptuous Blossom Revercomb, a vulnerable girl. Sarah's deceased husband, for whom she has long scrimped for the satisfaction of wearing real black crepe, was one of the "po' white trash." This discouraged class was long unable to compete with free black slave labor; now, however, black and white workers are being paid for their labor and there is hope for people of the Revercomb class to bestir themselves. The admixture of Sarah's obstinacy in the family blood promises to breed a new, vigorous type. Of her three sons, brooding Abner and shuffling Archie are all dull Revercomb, reverting back to the fecklessness of their father's kind. Abel alone inherits his mother's strength.

Abel loves Molly Merryweather, the hitherto unacknowledged illegitimate offspring of the decadent Gays. Old Jonathan Gay was murdered for seducing Molly's mother; some think his spirit ranges about the place at the "Ha'nts' Walk." As a love-child, Molly is chary of giving her affection. Thinking that Molly will never marry him, Abel resignedly transfers his passion to politics.

But he makes the mistake of engaging in a loveless match with plain, intense Judy Hatch, who herself secretly burns for another. This is the foppish Reverend Orlando Mullen, for whom she has been embroidering violet velvet slippers. Abel's and Judy's is an ashen marriage; they live alienated despite the intimacy of cohabitation, for their union has been "founded upon the simple law of racial continuance." Abel feels like a trapped animal but struggles to make the best of things, even when Judy tearfully confesses her love for Mullen. Judy fortuitously dies in premature labor, brought on by her frenzied belief that Mullen was dragged to death by a horse. Abel's freedom sobers him. Molly finally comes to him of her own accord. Abel's story thus deals with the fluctuations of his love affair with Molly and his ability to redirect his violent feeling to socially useful ends. Both he and Molly will give themselves to marriage, refined as they have been by experience and self-knowledge.

Molly is a focal figure in the novel, since in her veins runs the "riotous Gay blood," together with that of the humble Merryweathers. Her self-centered levity and flirtatiousness are attributable to her Gay ancestry. Yet, conscious of her mother's fall, Molly is fiercely chaste. Her dislike of "that kind of thing" enables her to assess her situation coolly. Like a wilderness creature, she fears being caged by marriage:

The sense of bondage would follow—on his part the man's effort to dominate; on hers the woman's struggle for the integrity of personality.

Her decision to remain aloof is reinforced by the terms of Jonathan Gay's will. Her true father, he had wished her to be a lady. Molly is left an income, provided she lives with the Gays. Her grandfather's death frees Molly to make her choice, and she goes to Jordan's Journey to acquire elegant ways. There she becomes aware of the Gay greed and selfishness. Her character deepens. She reflects that she has been able to sow her "mental wild oats," and she gains in wisdom. She appreciates now the worth of Abel, noble though rustic in manners, and accepts marriage with him.

Of the three families, the Gays are the powerful exploiters. Sensual Jonathan comes home to repeat his uncle's conduct and fate—the ill treatment of a poor white woman, for which he will be slain. For Jonathan desires lovely Blossom Revercomb. Her chaste upbringing will not allow her to yield without marriage; Gay marries her clandestinely and then cruelly tires of her. He never will acknowledge the match for fear of "murdering" his mother, a self-styled invalid. Abandoning Blossom, Jonathan openly pursues Molly, now his acknowledged cousin. Molly rejects him but commiserates with Blossom. Shame-faced Jonathan observes their sisterly embrace, recognizing the depth of "the need of woman for woman." Pathetic Blossom is last seen gliding like a ghost and watching from behind the tiger lilies as her careless husband gallops along the turnpike after another woman.

In the Gay family are two types of the Southern lady—the tyrant and the victim. Jonathan's mother, Miss Angela, is a lovely, fragile, iron-willed invalid. Her so-called heart attacks hold her family in subjection. Their respect for her health, declining for many vigorous years now, prevents any of them from living for themselves. And yet, Angela has outlived several who have feared for her well-being, all the while destroying their happiness both openly and secretly.

Among Angela's acts of inhumanity are her refusal to acknowledge her brother-in-law's, Jonathan Gay's, paternity of Molly, and her having prevented him from marrying the girl he ruined.

Angela has also wronged her own sister, Kesiah. Born plain, Kesiah was thought to be cut out for spinsterhood in a society that bred women for love. Kesiah, the misfit, had a painter's gift when young and had hoped to study. Angela helped to thwart that hope:

"Why should a girl want to go streaking across the water to study art . . . when she had a home she could stay in and men folk who could look after her?"

So Kesiah was sacrificed, her artist's aspirations stifled. By the time she had achieved her majority and financial independence, it was too late. The fight had gone out of her. Both women, delicate Angela and homely, submissive Kesiah, are "genuine products of the code of beautiful behaviour"[5] that deformed them as women and warped their human development.

The Gays are not landed aristocrats but newcomers to Jordan's Journey, which they bought from its previous owners. They have, however, assumed seigneurial rights over the resentful community, both in restricting hunting prerogatives long enjoyed by the poorer men, and in the graver matter of preying on their women. Adding to the injury, the Gay ladies have tarnished the names and perpetuated the misery of those same women. Morally, the Gays possess little that is truly fine or worth saving. Their best energy descends to Molly, free-spirited, impulsive, capable of refinement through experience. Through her, the verve of the Gay blood will join with the inherent good qualities of the upright countryman, Abel.

The aristocracy's selfish exploitation of the humbler whites as well as the weaker members of their own class signals the novel's concern with a breakdown in human relationships. This breakdown extends to the commerce between the sexes as well. The principal doings in *The Miller of Old Church* are courtships, weddings, seductions, and illicit passions across class and matrimonial lines. All that happens is precipitated by love, but most of these loves are ill-fated and unrequited, causing selfishness, perfidy, despair, insanity, hatred, murder. Marriages are unhappy, including that of the Revercombs' two comic grannies, competing to the death over their food and digestion.

At the Revercombs' and elsewhere there is a running commentary on courtship and marriage, usually in a humorous, epigrammatic style that defines these institutions as undesirable: "The chief thing lacking in marriage is conversation." When Abel tells his mother he is about to marry she interrupts him to order the hired man to "throw another spadeful of manure on that bridal wreath bush by the door." The Reverend Orlando Mullen gives his special sermon. Matrimony, he declares is founded upon sacrifice, the wife's: "Self-sacrifice was the breath in the nostrils of the womanly woman." His theme corroborates Molly's suspicion that marriage is "all work and no play."

Much of the commentary on the sexes takes place at the local pub, Bottom's Ordinary, a gathering and gossiping place. The pithy dialect of country people is a technique at which Glasgow excels; nowhere does she do it better than in this novel. The rustics meet to comment shrewdly on what is happening, serving as a chorus, providing exposition, and undeceiving one another on marriage. Betsey Bottom presides, a savory character full of mother wit. Having married a man she can manage, Betsey descants on the convenience of a "slue-footed," "slack-kneed" husband who can fill a space by the chimney.

Marriages motivated by the craving for domination or the perpetuation of the race are doomed. The best matches are those in which selfish impulses have been tamed. The forthcoming union of Molly and Abel that the novel's closing anticipates will combine the best their respective hereditary strengths have to transmit to the new South. The novel contains an important feature of the genre of romance, the founding of a better social order.

The work has its imperfections. Too often the narrative ploddingly directs the reader's attention to the hero's excellence and his mission in saving the region. His actual achievement is squeezed into the final pages, which report his political speech. Glasgow also initiates characterizations but fails to probe them after preparing the reader's expectations. She raises interest in Blossom Revercomb, her background, her clandestine marriage. Once Blossom is betrayed, however, the author drops her, letting her become another ghost like those drifting along Ha'nts' Walk. Judy Hatch is a potentially rich figure whom Glasgow handles confusedly. She explores Judy, then satirizes her, then conveniently kills her off in a half-comic episode, while also trying to give her some Darwinian pathos as one of the swarms of individuals whom nature squanders. Considering the novel's pervading antimatrimonial message, one is startled to come to the happy ending, a marriage to which Abel demands that the independent Molly give herself completely.

The work manages to transcend its faults, however, and it marks an important turning point in Glasgow's growth as a novelist. It is the most confi-

dently written, the most unified of the early works in
terms of character and society. The author succeeds
in her analysis of Molly as a fusion of heredity and
circumstance while realizing her as a plausible personality. She develops the sinister social implications
of Angela's willful innocence. The influencing role of
Sarah as the Calvinist mother is well integrated; she
is more than an amusing excresence like Mag Buzzy
in *The Ancient Law,* whom she resembles. Glasgow's
cynical humor about marriage is delightfully un-
strained. With their pastoral matings and mismat-
ings, peasantry and aristocracy are caught in the web
of their shared past and create a stylized Southern
rural microcosm. *The Miller of Old Church* makes
for fresh engaging reading, the best so far of Glasgow's works.

6

○○○○○○○○○○○○○○○○○○○○○○○○○○○○○○○○○

Virginia Heroines:

Virginia (1913),
Life and Gabriella (1916),
Barren Ground (1925)

While her beloved sister Cary lay dying of cancer in 1911, Glasgow had begun to sketch out her first novel of a Virginia heroine. *Virginia* was inspired by her mother, that "perfect flower of Southern culture" upon whose memory she brooded at Cary's bedside. *Life and Gabriella* followed in 1916. Some nine years later, *Barren Ground* appeared, which Glasgow considered her major achievement at that time, a work into which she felt her life's energies and genius had been poured.

In each novel, Glasgow creates a Southern woman whose development and suffering are precipitated by a marriage or relationship with a man less worthy than she. Also implicit in each novel is an ideal of feminine behavior that helps to form the heroine or against which she must contend. Virginia Pendleton, growing up in the post-war South of the 1880s, is a young woman of genteel family. She becomes submerged and defeated in her marriage to a successful playwright. Gabriella Carr, coming from a similar background a decade later, is abandoned by her dissolute husband but cultivates a working life for herself and rears her children alone. Glasgow thought of Virginia and Gabriella as companion portraits. Dorinda Oakley, the heroine of *Barren Ground*, a country girl from the bleak Piedmont region, is seduced by an unstable country doctor in her

village. She loses her child during pregnancy, fore-
swears love, and learns to live as successful farmer
and landowner "without happiness." The progres-
sion from Virginia to Gabriella to Dorinda is from a
woman married and committed to her three children, to a divorced working woman with two children, to a resolutely unmarried, childless woman.
Each heroine, as a Southern woman, expresses something of what Glasgow felt about the South with all
its tragedy, beauty, and capacity for survival. Even
more pertinently, these novels are rich in the discourse of feminism. They reveal Glasgow's deep understanding of the woman's lot, regardless of time
and place, as she deals with power and powerless-
ness, love, maternity, isolation, and work.

Virginia (1913)

After Cary's death, Glasgow left her aged father in his
nurse's care and took an apartment in New York on
Central Park West. Traveling at intervals between
New York and Richmond, she completed *Virginia* in
less than two years. She dedicated it to Cary's memory. Although she had originally meant "to deal ironically with both the Southern lady and Victorian tradition, I discovered, as I went on, that my irony grew
fainter, while it yielded at last to sympathetic compas-
sion." An affectionate exposure of the retrograde
South, *Virginia* is about the girl and the place:

I could not separate Virginia from her background, because she was an integral part of it, and it shared her valid-
ity.

The work moves beyond region and period, however, achieving a universal importance in its depic-
tion of women's condition. Virginia conforms to "the

feminine ideal of the ages," rooted in tradition that "had sprung from the dreams of Adam, and had been preserved in the eternal forms of religion and legend."[1]

Virginia's story of courtship, marriage and desertion is divided into three parts: "The Dream," "The Reality," and "The Adjustment."

In "The Dream," Virginia Pendleton is a lovely, romantic girl of nineteen. She has grown up in Dinwiddie, which represents Petersburg. Her background and education are dwelt upon at length. Her father, an idealistic Episcopal minister, had fought in the Civil War. Her mother is a lady whom poverty has chastened. Lucy Pendleton's look is one of "pathetic cheerfulness." Her husband imagines that she enjoys toiling for his sake. Her once beautiful hands are gnarled with work. Virginia looks upon her mother's life supposing that her own will be vastly different.

She and her friend Susan Treadwell—who is as competent as Virginia is clinging—are first seen as white-gowned girls in the garden of their school. Susan remains a lifelong foil to Virginia, for Susan decides that her happiness will not depend on any man. Their schoolmistress is Miss Priscilla Batte, a dignified relict of the educational principle that "the less a girl knew about life, the better prepared she would be to contend with it. . . . Learning was to be kept from her as rigorously as if it contained the germs of a contagious disease." Ignorance would guarantee a young woman's desirability to a worldly, knowledgeable man.

Such negative education is especially valued in a patriarchal society that remains socially conservative. Industrially, however, the town develops in order to survive. Miss Priscilla stands for all that is regressive in the New South. An anachronism in the midst of progress, Miss Priscilla stands "firmly rooted in all that was static, in all that was obsolete and outgrown in the Virginia of the eighties."

As Priscilla represents the town's past, the man who is most important to its future is Cyrus Treadwell, Susan's father. He is Dinwiddie's industrial leader, president of the railroad, builder of the tobacco industry, owner of interests in lumber and cotton. But as the town's commercial savior, Treadwell has less interest in relieving the downtrodden than in treading profitably upon them. His personal relationships with family and dependent blacks reveal his cruelty.

Treadwell's nephew, Oliver, an aspiring playwright, comes to town. Oliver and Virginia mistake their youthful desire for love, although they are scarcely acquainted. Waiting for Oliver at a dance, Virginia has a glimmering of what love may mean for a woman:

Was that a woman's life, after all? Never to be able to go out and fight for what one wanted! Always to sit at home and wait, without moving a foot or lifting a hand toward happiness! . . . Always to will in secret, always to hope in secret, always to triumph or to fail in secret.

But she thrusts these doubts aside. Oliver prepares to sacrifice his literary hopes to support a wife.

In "The Reality," Virginia is readied for marriage in a flurry of dressmaking and precepts about self-sacrifice. Fixed in her mother's mind are

the archaic roots of her inherited belief in the Pauline measure of her sex.[2] It was characteristic of her—and indeed of most women of her generation—that she would have endured martyrdom in support of the consecrated doctrine of her inferiority to man.

She transmits this wisdom to her daughter. On reading the marriage service Virginia wonders, "What could be more beautiful or more sacred . . . ? What could make her happier than the knowledge that she must surrender her will to his from the day of her wedding until the day of her death?"

The first years of marriage are wittily documented in Virginia's naively bright-spirited letters, through which disillusionment seeps like a stain. She writes home from Matoaca City, a mining town in which the newly wedded husband finds employment. The bloom of passion is soon off the marriage as four children are born in rapid succession, one dying in infancy. Virginia devotes herself utterly to them and to her housewifery. She neglects her person, supposing, like a number of Glasgow's misguided wives, that Oliver doesn't have "that side to his nature." Seven years of marriage leave her dowdy, motherly, older-looking than the radiant, well-dressed Oliver.

The marriage palls on Oliver. Virginia's domesticity, her attention is for the children rather than for him, and his disappointed hopes of a serious literary career, impell him to cast about for happiness. He writes popular plays that take him frequently to New York. Virginia cannot talk with her husband about his work, but she darns his socks. "As a wife Virginia was perfect; as a mental companion, she barely existed at all." Her solicitude is cloying. Her beauty wastes. She sees her work-worn hands, like her mother's, "but a single pair in that chain of pathetic hands that had worked in the exacting service of Love." During a diphtheria crisis, Virginia nurses her child to health while her petulant, pleasure-loving husband joins an excursion to Atlantic City. She feels herself, like her own mother and the line of women before her, a participant in the "immemorial pang of motherhood." Her agony as she bends over the child's bed forces her to renounce once and for all any personal wish or vanity and to close the door definitively on her youth.

In "The Adjustment" Virginia mourns for her father, brutally killed in a lynching incident. Her mother's death, rendered in an excellent vignette, follows. Virginia is thirty and considers her life over. Oliver at thirty-five is hale and youthful. "And, like other men who have lived day by day with heroically unselfish women, he had fallen at last into the habit of thinking that his being comfortable was, after all, a question of supreme importance to the universe."

By the time Virginia is forty-five, Oliver's success has purchased material comforts for all the family. Having outgrown their need of her, the children are indifferent to their faded, uninteresting mother. Her independent daughters, competently managing their lives, are made to seem cold beside her. The bond between mother and daughters is ruptured by their new feminism.

Oliver now spends much of the year in New York with his fascinating mistress, Margaret Oldcastle, an actress of talent and intelligence. Faced with the empty nest of home, Virginia is idle. When the children were small she had considered the least diversion a guilty self-indulgence and consequently is not in the habit of doing anything enjoyable. Her sole pleasure with Oliver is of "supplying his food and of watching him eat it." Her principal achievement is in aiding Oliver's success:

She had laid her youth down on the altar of her love, while he had used love as he had used life, merely to feed the flame of the unconquerable egoism which burned like genius within him.

On a visit to New York Virginia learns of her husband's wild love for Margaret Oldcastle. She calls on the actress to talk to her, woman to woman. But once she faces that glowing personage she falters, unable to be candid.

The actress is sketched in Darwinian terms, as one who has survived at the expense of feebler women:

She stood not only for the elemental forces but for the free woman; and her freedom, like that of man, had been built upon the strewn bodies of the weaker. . . . The justice not of society, but of nature, was on her side, for she was one with evolution and with the resistless principle of change.

Virginia recognizes Margaret's superior natural force, against which her own civilized, socially conditioned submissiveness is helpless. "She realized she was fighting not a woman, but a structure of life." In evolutionary terms, it is as if the cultivated spirit of proud sacrifice has been bred in the bone of Virginia and her kind, to the extent that it is now an acquired characteristic that has become inherent.

Willing to remain in the hell she has helped to create, Virginia grants her husband a divorce. She treats him as tenderly as if he were a sick child. The novel ends with her looking both to the past and the future. She revisits scenes of youthful happiness, especially the changeless blossoming garden of her girlhood. She also waits expectantly for her son's return from Oxford. His letter, "Dearest Mother, I am coming back to you," provides the closing note of irony. Virginia, unable to save herself, must still look for a hero on the horizon. Implicit is the echo of her younger reflections upon the woman's role: "Always to sit at home and wait." The promise of coming back does not announce the return of Oliver, toward whom she has become motherly, but instead a male rescuer of the future generation.

The aggressive Treadwells and selfless Pendletons symbolize for Glasgow two ways of life for the South, both of which she regards with some ambiva-

lence. The builder-destroyer Cyrus is a morally am-
biguous figure, useful but repellent. The gracious,
self-immolating, foolish Pendletons are viewed
elegiacally. Glasgow found it hard to dismiss the old,
generous, mannerly ways of the sheltered world in
which she had grown up. Virginia is herself, in some
ways, the South. Cruelly used, she has stood for morality, beauty, tradition. She has been defeated but
not destroyed. As representatives of the "new"
Treadwells and the "old" Pendletons, Oliver and Virginia are in Glasgow's evolutionary scheme the survivor and the victim.

"The Treadwells had always stood for success."
For Susan, success meant her independence, for
Cyrus it was power and wealth, for Oliver it was his
art. Oliver uses Virginia and then abandons her for
Margaret. He and Margaret suit each other, since
each is committed to self-aggrandizement at the expense of the weak. In both of them, the "structure of
life" has bred the natural instinct to adapt and survive. They are the force of the future.

Tradition is served by the Pendletons. Devoted
to ancestral ideals of virtue and altruism, they uphold
these to their own detriment. In them, civilization
has nurtured the will to loving sacrifice, which they
practice in daily rituals of politeness and self-denial.
All three Pendletons ultimately play sacrificial roles,
giving their lives for others. Virginia willingly offers
her whole feminine being to the continuance of the
race, though growing in self-awareness as she does in
unhappiness. At the last, cognizant of her plight, she
is incapable of change; the principle of sacrifice has,
through heredity and training, been infused in her
blood. The course of Virginia's life is dictated by her
link to the atavistic chain of mothers, whose toil-
knotted hands betoken their love-service. Mother to
the race, to her children, to her husband even, she

affirms her bond with all mothers—her own or the woman on the street.

Despite her seeming indictment of the Southern lady, Glasgow maintained that Virginia is not to be understood as weak. Rather, she was "a woman whose vital energy had been deflected, by precept and example, into a single emotional centre."[3] In this sacrifice women are abetted by male vanity. Oliver's youthful views about women receive satirical attention. He has been accustomed to thinking of "the primal necessity of woman, not as an individual, but as an incentive and an appendage to the dominant personality of man." The allure of marriage is that it enables him to go forth into the world while a sacrificial womanly woman is "at home waiting—always waiting, with those eyes like wells of happiness, until he should return to her!" His maturer thoughts as a married man bored with his wife are a logical outgrowth of his youthful prejudices: "He saw woman as dependent upon man for the very integrity of her being, and beyond the divine fact of this dependency, he did not see her at all."

In differentiating between the sexes, Glasgow also ironically presents for the reader's consideration the common view that women live entirely for love while men do not. For women "love is the supreme occupation of being"; for man it is "at best a partial manifestation of energy." But sexual love, like everything else, is always available to men:

All life was for men, and only a few radiant years of it were given to women. Men were never too old to love, to pursue and capture whatever joy the fugitive instant might hold for them.

In *Virginia* the writing is perfectly controlled, poised between authorial involvement and detachment. Unlike some of the earlier novels, where doctrines of culture and biology obtrude, this work represents a masterful fusion of ideas with felt life. Patriarchal culture, religion, principles of female education, and Southern gentility conspire with the law of species to devour the heroine. Nor does Glasgow indulge in sentimental oversimplification. The heroine begins by acquiescing in her destruction and then is allowed to observe its progress without being able to extricate herself. *Virginia* is one of Glasgow's finest works, as well as an American naturalist novel of major importance. Overshadowed by other of her novels of less distinction because of its inaccessibility, it merits being restored to the curriculum.

Life and Gabriella (1916)

After the publication of *Virginia,* Glasgow went to Europe and was back in July 1914, just before the outbreak of World War I. On her return she took up residence in her Central Park West apartment, where she went to work on her next book, much of it set in New York.

Still interested in that female dedication of energy she had explored in *Virginia,* Glasgow creates a heroine to contrast with Virginia Pendleton. Gabriella Carr is not beautiful; more importantly, she is intelligent and purposeful. The book's subtitle is "The Story of a Woman's Courage." As a "vein of iron" woman, Gabriella can survive without the aid of the husband who deserts her. Living just ten years after Virginia, Gabriella finds herself in a changed era. No longer is the Southern woman compelled to exist "chiefly as an ornament to civilization."[4] Gabriella discovers her reserves of strength as she passes from innocence to experience in the two parts of the novel: "The Age of Faith" and "The Age of Knowledge."

Gabriella lives in post–Civil War Richmond with her querulous widowed mother and her married, separated, sister Jane. Jane's degrading marriage, like the unions in *The Wheel of Life,* stands as a warning of matrimonial dangers. The helplessness of the mother and sister is thrown into relief by the esteem in which they hold the male sex. Mrs. Carr, especially, endures her genteel poverty while fashioning lampshades and waiting "patiently for some man to come and support her." The rescuer might be a husband for Gabriella. In the meantime, Gabriella obtains employment in a shop, a step that evokes well-mannered horror.

As a saleswoman in Brandywine and Plummer she learns the lucrative art of millinery. The vignette of this commercial establishment represents Glasgow at her comic best. The shop is staffed with impoverished gentlewomen, the daughters of Civil War heroes. Far from being a vulgar emporium, it is a sanctuary for distressed ladies with the hushed atmosphere of a convent. Each counter is presided over by a woman of impeccable genealogy and manners. Each woman is noted for the battle in which her heroic father fell, or the plantation from which she descended. To do one's shopping at Brandywine and Plummer was to be waited on by some of the highest blood in Virginia.

George Fowler, a Southerner living in New York, comes wooing Gabriella and she yields eagerly to him. Their courtship is handled with irony. George is taken aback by Gabriella's amorous abandon, but he tolerates it while not giving as much:

In one thing, however, they were passionately agreed, and that was that the aim and end of their marriage was to make George perfectly happy. . . . Women did love more than men, he supposed, but what else were they here for?

George dislikes independence in women. He welcomes Gabriella's seeming renunciation of her will for his sake. Should not woman, he reflects, "be content to lay down not only her life but her very identity for love?" Gabriella falls into the snare of this fowler. Entrapped, she clings to George with passionate folly and accepts everything, including the requirement that they live in New York with his parents. But in the early years of the marriage George's vices become apparent. A profligate with money, women, and drink, he swiftly tires of Gabriella.

By the beginning of the novel's second part, Gabriella has a daughter and a son. George has left her for another woman. Gabriella at twenty-seven has reached the end of her delusions about love. Hardened, she rejects her mother-in-law's facile philosophy—that men are variable but women in their hearts will go on loving no matter what. The new Gabriella declares: "Marriage isn't made for love. I used to think it was—but it isn't—" After obtaining a divorce she resolves to turn to work for support and solace.

She secures a position in the fashionable Maison Dinard as a saleswoman and milliner. Madame Dinard, née O'Brady, stands as a fearsome warning of what the self-made independent married woman may become. Having supported six children and three of her four husbands, Madame is an ancient and wheezing matron, corseted, painted, dyed, autocratic, and indomitable.

Gabriella by day is a vision of pale austere ele-

gance in black, exactly suited to the fashionable
world she serves. Her femininity is not so frail as
before. At home, she has three modest rooms, sharing kitchen and bath with some student tenants in an
apartment on the city's West side near Columbus
Avenue. Her old garrulous dressmaker from Richmond comes up north to care for the children. When
a suitor presents himself, Gabriella declares she has
"had enough of marriage to last me a lifetime."

Gabriella eventually buys her way into the Dinard business. She has to turn for advice and a loan
to a social acquaintance, the elderly, ugly Judge
Crowborough. He agrees to help, then takes the opportunity to embrace her. Gabriella, enraged and
disgusted, silently reiterates a thought she has had
before: Women need to be beautiful, men need only
be rich and powerful:

The stupendous, the incredible vanity of man!—she reflected disdainfully. Was there ever a man too ugly, too
repulsive, or too old to delude himself with the belief that
he might still become the object of passion?

Calmly she indicates she would prefer to be treated
"as a gentleman."

At thirty-seven, Gabriella has lived ten years
without a man. She moves to a new neighborhood,
London Terrace, in New York's old Chelsea. She
becomes physically attracted to her neighbor, Ben
O'Hara. Ungrammatical, red-headed Ben has a large
experience of the rugged world of men. He has been
from Bonanza City to the Bowery. When, surprisingly, a derelict Fowler lurches home to Gabriella to
die a drunkard's death, O'Hara takes over both the
deathbed and funeral arrangements. Grateful and
admiring, Gabriella decides that O'Hara is for her.
After a flying trip to Richmond to ascertain that her
family and old friends really do seem hopelessly be-

nighted, corrupt, or effete, she returns to New York
to catch up with O'Hara at the train station. She
promises to marry him that night, breathlessly vowing "I'll come with you now—anywhere—toward the
future."

Life and Gabriella proved a popular book,
achieving fifth place on the bestseller list for 1916. In
the opening portions of the novel, Glasgow succeeds
in spinning her customary satire in dealing with the
fallen gentry of postwar Richmond. However, with
Gabriella her sense of irony forsakes her. As she
grows deeply involved in her heroine's tribulations,
she fails to maintain a distanced control over her
subject, dwelling upon Gabriella's innate refinement, her perfections.

Especially heavy-handed are Glasgow's praises
of Gabriella's female and racial excellences at the
expense of other characters. Where Gabriella is aristocratic, other women are "overdressed," "cheap,"
"common," or "pathetic." Gabriella's lack of beauty
is said to be preferable to the spoiled prettiness, the
"trite little face" of her daughter, whose "mind
. . . was small and trite like her face." Her secure
social position gives her an edge over vulgar Madame
Dinard with her thin credentials. The author speaks
of "the finer attributes which Nature had bred in her
race," deprecating the "lethargic foreign faces beside her finer American type." Gabriella is of "hardy
stock" and inherits her father's "fighting spirit," superior to the masses of the immigrant population of
New York.

Glasgow's insistence on her heroine's preemi-
nence was undoubtedly intended to demonstrate
how a woman's courage could sustain her in a world
not friendly to energetic, unbeautiful women. Her
eagerness to celebrate the spirited resolves of the
strongest Southern women (tied to her views about

the South's capacity to reassert itself) led her to deal boldly and astutely with questions of women's personal freedom. What keeps Gabriella going is the sense that she has the "right to be happy, but it depends on myself."

Throughout, the novel develops its voluminous discourse on the rivalry between the sexes, the dispraise of masculine vanity and selfishness, the praise of women who work and win. The discourse is revelatory of how much thought Glasgow gave to such questions as women's feelings of their own worth, their decisions about how they should lead their lives, the importance of loving men, and the resentment against depending on that love. The novel offers numerous sketches of women compelled by life or coping with it: the ill-married, the well-married, the spinster, the kept woman, the tough self-made married woman, the cowed and dependent mother-in-law, the flirtatious suffragette. In many ways, Glasgow's commentary is today more interesting than the narrative, pointedly addressing as it does issues of perennial concern to women.

In the matter of work, it is as if Glasgow posed the problem: What shall the ordinary, intelligent woman do to survive? The work Gabriella does is not in itself fulfilling but is only a means to her independence. It is also work that enables her to retain her ladylike status, her "charm"; millinery and fashion are feminine undertakings. In fact, after her early novels about women artists, discussed above in Chapter 2, none of Glasgow's working women are dedicated professionals. They are nurse-companions, decorators, or secretaries, doing jobs that are secondary to their womanly concerns of love. So too with Gabriella. She labors long hours to maintain a gracious, even "consecrated" home atmosphere for her children. Motherhood and ultimately the hope of marriage once again absorb her more deeply than work. Despite the pervasive hostility expressed toward men, in the hasty concluding episodes solid Gabriella will again grow girlish and be whirled off her feet by a stereotypically virile man. She seems about to make the same mistake twice. Her acceptance of O'Hara negates her own achievements in supporting her children, for O'Hara contemptuously disparages the rearing of male children by their mothers, who would make them into "muffs" and "mollycoddles." The novel's conclusion implies that if women want love they have to be willing to yield up autonomy, work that is intrinsically important, and the pleasures of significant achievement.

Glasgow admitted that soon after she had finished *Life and Gabriella* she "let go and gave up." Her work for the next seven years was inconsequential. During that period she published two minor novels centering on political heroes, *The Builders* (1919) and *One Man in His Time* (1922). In 1923 she collected and brought out a volume of her short stories. Then, with renewed inspiration and energy, she "boiled up . . . out of those depths" and embarked upon what she expected would be her best work.[5]

Barren Ground (1925)

Here was a new, elemental woman. Not a lady, she differed from earlier genteel heroines who were subject to Victorian Virginian codes of feminine conduct and burdened by mothers and mentors with precepts appropriate to their class. Instead, Dorinda Oakley would be a female version of Glasgow's "plain man," sharing in the strength of the independent yeoman farmers. Her challenge would be not society but her sexual nature. Hers would be a life "amid the broomsedge [and] sassafras in the abandoned fields of Virginia."[6]

The novel's sections, each bearing the name of a plant, correspond to the phases of Dorinda Oakley's life. Part I, "Broomsedge," begins in 1894, when she is twenty. Part II, "Pine," takes her to her thirty-eighth year. Part III, "Life-Everlasting," the name of a plant that dries with a silvery blossom, moves from 1916 to 1924, when the heroine is fifty years old.

Dorinda comes of hard-toiling, land-poor folk. Her father has a stupified, animal look. Her mother, of austere Calvinist stock, is worn down by marriage, pain, work, and religiosity to the point of mental instability. Love is viewed askance by the Oakleys, for in the family annals there were female relatives whom love had maddened or destroyed. Yet Dorinda is eager for the kind of fulfillment she has glimpsed in books. Her romantic yearning fixes on a local object, an auburn-haired, citified young doctor named Jason Greylock. He has an alcoholic father. Dorinda mistakes desire for love, even religious exaltation. She fails to understand that her biological nature controls her: "The powers of life had seized her as an eagle seizes its prey."

The pair become engaged, then are lovers. Dorinda, finding herself pregnant, perceives the landscape as bleak and littered with decay, broken buildings, sick animals. Fainting, she sees fields of a weed called broomsedge, associated with her sexuality, apparently raging toward her and engulfing her. That night she discovers that Jason has married another girl, one he had courted the year before. Her menfolk have forced the marriage, and Jason confesses he was too "white-livered" to resist, despite his having compromised Dorinda.

Dorinda tries to kill Jason and fails. She thrusts aside all religion. Her soul is "parched and black-

ened, like an abandoned field after the broomsedge
is destroyed." Yet in her there is the unbreakable
"vein of iron". She leaves Pedlar's Mill, heading for
New York.

The dominant symbol of Part II is the enduring
harp-shaped pine tree that Dorinda will come morally to resemble. This pine, the highest in Queen
Elizabeth County, rises up out of a rocky soil in the
midst of the Oakleys' family graveyard, as if drawing
its vitality from the bones of the dead. From these
ancestors Dorinda inherits the strong will that sus-
tains her. The tree is a living link between their past
and her present.

In New York, Dorinda miscarries. She finds work
caring for a physician's office and for his children. She
refuses a suitor, declares herself "finished with love,"
and determines to fill her life with something better.
She suffers, however, from the pangs of the biological
nature she denies. At a concert she feels nervous
sensations of ecstasy, the music tearing at her and
torturing her.[7] Dreams of Jason haunt her. But she
will divert her energies from love to work, planning
to start a dairy farm.

Two years later she returns home. Back at Pedlar's Mill there is general hardship. Jason drinks and
neglects his practice. His wife becomes insane and
dies a suicide. Dorinda's father dies. Her brother kills
a man. Her mother gives false testimony to exoner-
ate him and is broken by the ordeal, dying soon after.

While others decline, Dorinda gathers strength,
lingering often for inspiration beneath the great ancestral pine. She acquires lands and cattle that once
belonged to rivals and enemies. She labors to grow
rich. The numbing physical routine subdues most of
her emotion. Only at night is she tormented by
dreams that betray sexual need. But toward Jason
himself, when he seeks reconciliation and forgive-

ness, she shows pitiless contempt, rejoicing in her hardness.

At thirty-three Dorinda enters into a business-like, unconsummated marriage with a homely store-keeper named Nathan Pedlar. Nathan helps Dorinda increase her land holdings. A satisfactory husband, he is like a "superior hired man on the farm." Dorinda succinctly puts her view of marriage: "Well, I won't let it interfere with my work. No man is going to do that."

Part III, "Life-Everlasting," opens with an account of the compatibility of Nathan, who is submissive, and Dorinda, who is authoritative. She is content with their nine loveless years of marriage. Then, at forty-two, Dorinda is widowed when Nathan dies heroically in a train accident. The town puts up a memorial, and Dorinda is not displeased with her role as a hero's widow. Meeting Jason again, Dorinda looks down at him from her white horse "like some mature Joan of Arc." Jason willingly admits her superiority and his own weakness and degeneracy.

We finally see Dorinda as a strong, comely woman of fifty. At the height of her prosperity, she is one day asked by neighbors to take in the indigent, tubercular Jason, his condition worsened by alcoholism. The neighbors point out that perhaps she owes him something, as she had once been able to buy his farm so cheaply. Quelling her indignation, she agrees to give him lodging to keep him from death in the poorhouse. She nurses Jason through a bout of hemorrhages until he dies. After his burial, Dorinda experiences a sense of renewal. Having put her life's energies into the land, and now her lover into the earth, she is able to draw sustenance from both in return. Her own electric vitality passes into the earth to mingle there, as it were, with her lover's body; the image is one of displaced sexuality. Their joined en-

ergies are transmitted through the earth to reenter
the woman, who now feels herself recharged with
cosmic energies. "The spirit of the land was flowing
into her, and her own spirit, strengthened and re-
freshed, was flowing out again toward life."

Barren Ground had a supremely personal importance for Glasgow. In part, the novel grew out of
the pain of her drawn-out love affair with Henry
Anderson. Writing it enabled her to confirm her renunciation of that love and reassert her commitment
to her life of work and independence. She wrote, "It
became for me . . . almost a vehicle of liberation." She
had lived close to Dorinda for a decade and had
borne the idea of the novel with her throughout that
time before devoting three years to its writing. It was
"the truest novel ever written"; it was "torn out of
myself." "I wrote *Barren Ground*, and immediately
I knew I had found myself."[8] The American reading
public was less enthusiastic about the stiff-necked
heroine, but literary critics acclaimed the work, not
without some reservations. James Branch Cabell
called it "the best of many excellent books by Ellen
Glasgow."[9] It was in this same review that he observed that her sixteen novels to date might be considered a "portrayal of all social and economic Virginia since the War Between the States."

Three themes help to explain the heroine's character. First, there is the feminist theme, conceived
here in the severe terms of a woman's determination
to live free of sexual entanglement and her vengeful
contentment at seeing her lover brought low. Second, there is the Calvinist theme, referring to the
heroine's "vein of iron" legacy from her staunch
Scotch-Irish forebears, the early settlers of the region. And third, there is the all-pervading agrarian
theme, that yearning toward the land that impels the
heroine to reaffirm her bond with it.

The feminist orientation of the novel takes up
from where Glasgow had left off in her earlier works
on Virginia heroines. Of *Barren Ground* she wrote:

For once, in Southern fiction, the betrayed woman would
become the victor instead of the victim. In the end she
would triumph through that deep instinct for survival,
which had ceased to be a negative quality and had
strengthened into a dynamic force.[10]

Dorinda does not sink into permanent despair after
being seduced and abandoned. Her capacity for survival enables her to gain control over her own body
and mind, over the earth, and finally over the man
who had destroyed her early happiness. She claims
she made the right choices, that married women are
less happy than she. It is assumed that the sexes are
mutually antagonistic. Dorinda observes that men
will impose on women when they can; she discerns
in "all men who were not milksops, the masculine
instinct to domineer over the opposite sex." She feels
the menace of her old lover: "He was buried somewhere in her consciousness, like a secret enemy who
could spring out of the wilderness and strike her
when she was defenseless."

When she is not feeling threatened by Jason, she
can grow scornful:

"Men were so immature . . . and they were never so immature as when they strutted most with importance."

It pleases her that she can be "cruel" toward pleading Jason.[11] She sees him as a "thing," her husband
as "a sick sheep." The male characters are feebly
drawn. Jason and Nathan are abject shadows who fail
to come to life and over whom Dorinda can easily
show her superiority.[12]

Glasgow has Dorinda make her decisions in defiance of the convention that prescribes marriage

and motherhood for women. Dorinda finds her
fulfillment, as Glasgow was herself determined to do,
through work. She repeatedly affirms her heroine's
will to live "without delight." Dorinda exclaims: "Oh
if the women who wanted love could only know the
infinite relief of having love over." The novel's last
words are her deprecating response to the hint that
she may one day remarry: "I am thankful to have
finished with all that."

    Dorinda's Calvinist heritage has much to do with
her mistrust of sexual love. Her Bible-reading
mother had been lured into love by her young, poor-
white husband's resemblance to a John the Baptist.[13]
She had then become disillusioned. While rejecting
her parents' traditional Christian beliefs and their
unconscious emulation of martyrs' roles, Dorinda
converts the Calvinist attitudes of her forebears into
a working philosophy. "The moral fibre that had stiff-
ened the necks of the martyrs lay deeply embedded
in her character if not in her opinions." She reflects
on her birthright:

She had inherited, she realized, the religious habit of mind
without the religious heart; . . . Firmness of purpose, independence of character, courage of living, these attributes
she had gleaned from these heavy furrows of her great-
grandfather's sowing.[14]

The energy that Dorinda summons throughout is
owing not only to her efforts but also to the family
legacy of fortitude. More fit for survival, Dorinda has
in this respect the Darwinian advantage over the
"degenerate" Jason. From her "vein of iron" ancestors, Dorinda derives her portion of the Protestant
ethic: the "inner-directedness," the immersion in
work, the identification of prosperity with salvation,
the sense of being one of the "elect." These qualities
enable her to stand starkly alone, to shun all human

relationships except those that help her to prosper. Maxwell Geismar, generally admiring of Glasgow, demurs critically: "For all the emphasis on moral virtues," what *Barren Ground* really achieves is a "study of thwarted and twisted emotions . . . driven underground."[15] In many respects the heroine's stern feminism and her Calvinist legacy reinforce each other.

It is perhaps through the agrarian metaphor that Glasgow most consistently defines Dorinda and elevates her above the human fray to an almost mythic status. For whereas Dorinda stifles her humanity, she shares in the rhythms of the seasons and rejoices in the fruits of her labors. In this she fulfills her role of the idealized farmer, long glorified in the legends of the South.[16] For Glasgow, *Barren Ground* signalled a return to a rural setting like that of her early Virginia novels:

I had known that I must return to the familiar earth in which I was rooted and to the earlier fibres of my identity, which reached far down into a past that was deeper and richer than conscious recollection.[17]

In this yearning toward the land, Glasgow was also expressing a sentiment that was discernible among Southerners from World War I on—disenchantment with the rise of the industrial New South and nostalgia for an agrarian past. There had always been an element of resistance to this industrialization. Now, the hastening of production to serve the world war's needs, the mass movement to cities, and the abandonment of small farms were propelling the entire region suddenly toward modern industrial capitalism. The rampant business ethic, the reverence for money, for the smokestack, and the machine, were felt to pose a threat to the old tranquil values of a landed gentry. These changes meant embracing busy, hard-boiled Yankee ways, and proclaimed a kind of treachery against the neglected land. Progress became identified with mechanization, depersonalization, even corruption. A way of staving off the urban encroachment seemed to be to reaffirm the life of the province and the farm.

   Barren Ground is an epic of the soil. Dorinda sees herself and her parents as products of earth: "Had not the land entered their souls and shaped their moods into permanent or impermanent forms?" Dorinda's own emotional life is a "buried jungle." Her dreams are haunted by Jason-faced thistles, which she struggles to plough up. Broomsedge, pine, and life-everlasting refer to the flora of the soul, those she manages to root out and those she will nurture. Her conquest of the land is symbolic of her energetic control of her biological and passional nature.

   Broomsedge, an overly persistent image, runs like "smothered fire over the melancholy brown of the landscape." Farmers burn it, but it comes back. An old rustic comments, "Broomsedge ain't jest wild stuff. It's a kind of fate." Described as the "wild, free principle in nature," it is the "smothered fire" in Dorinda's veins: It enters her hallucinations when she discovers her pregnancy; it parches her spirit; it haunts her sexual dreams.

   As she grows older, Dorinda becomes identified with other forms of growth. The harp-shaped pine of ancestral endurance rises high above the broomsedge. The surname "Oakley" suggests the same solidity, in contrast to the pastoral "Dorinda," implying her youthful romanticism. As a handsome old woman, her face is "rough and hard like the rind of winter fruit." In the prime of age she rides among "the silver gleams which flashed up from the life-everlasting." The flowers' "white fire" mirrors victorious Dorinda's cloud of white hair.

Dorinda Oakley emerges as Glasgow's most self-reliant and isolated heroine, the one who is most cynically disdainful of love. "Three months of love," she muses, "and you pay for it with the rest of your life." Rendered permanently numbed to sexual love, she is also incapable of any human involvement. Her relationships with the novel's flattened characters—mother, father, brothers, lover, rival, husband—are one sided, serving chiefly to point up her own struggles and triumphs where other mortals falter.

With her lifelong habit of sublimating emotion and sinking herself in her work, her rejection of human ties, her deep scorn of others' frailty, her defensive conviction that she is right, Dorinda remains a potentially fascinating figure. Her stifled sexuality and her obsession with vengeance against so capsized a foe as Jason would make her a worthy subject of penetrating psychological scrutiny. But Glasgow fails to seize this opportunity. Too involved personally in Dorinda's ascendancy to see her neuroses plainly, Glasgow is unable to maintain the necessary ironic distance to judge her. Where Dorinda is repressed and vindictive, Glasgow insists she is serenely strong. Where Dorinda is deadened, her author thinks her alive. Unwilling to come to terms fully with her heroine's impaired humanity, Glasgow believes to the end, as Dorinda herself does, in her moral superiority. To retrieve her from her human quandaries, the author transforms her into a saintly or mythic figure—a Joan of Arc with a mission, a spouse and sister to the earth. "Kinship with the land was filtered through the blood and into the brain." Her sexuality is at the last neutralized. Earth's forces flow into her, while her own energies flow outward to nature.

Barren Ground succeeds as a rich regional novel, with earth symbolizing the body of the heroine. It is perhaps the work for which Glasgow is best known, and it has never gone out of print. But the novel's fame has not served the author's reputation well. Although, polemically, the novel provides lively fuel to the flames of sexual politics, its overstated female anger mars it artistically. The renown of *Barren Ground* has caused it to eclipse the superior *Virginia,* in which the same anger is delicately refined and controlled. Most contemporary critics have been forced, reluctantly, to admit that the vision of *Barren Ground* is conflicted and faulty. Dorinda is too much a *tour de force* as the betrayed woman victorious, trampling on her undoer; the iron-veined Calvinist, laying up treasures but despairing forever of earthly joy; and the mythic, golden-age laborer, kin to and wedded to the soil, affirming the old agrarian values, forcibly bringing her human drives into consonance with the rhythms of the cosmos.

7

○○○○○○○○○○○○○○○○○○○○○○○○○○○○○○

Changing Times and Sexual Mores:
The Romantic Comedians (1926),
They Stooped to Folly (1929),
The Sheltered Life (1932)

Once she completed *Barren Ground,* which had filled her with "the sense of the tragic life,"[1] Glasgow felt the need for laughter. She was in her fifties; she had unburdened in that novel her angry disappointment at having finished with love and was now able to treat the relations between the sexes satirically. Her major trilogy of manners was set in Queenborough, her name for a heightened version of Richmond that was "the distilled essence of all Virginia cities." In Queenborough she saw an anachronistic effort to maintain "a code of beautiful behaviour" while the rest of the world grew more uncivilized. But even Queenborough must also succumb to changing times and the new morality, which, for Glasgow meant the "craving for the raw taste of life, for the sight and savour of blood, for the brutal ferocity of lust without love."[2] This rather overwrought statement about what the novels treat with cool Olympian irony refers to a pre– and post–World War I sexual revolution.

Changes in sexual mores affect women more than men; the Queenborough novels are filled with female characters. Each Queenborough novel has also its old Virginia gentleman—a judge, a lawyer, and a general, respectively—who belongs to the courtly school of the nineteenth century. A lifelong

admirer of womanly graces, he surveys a bewildering
array of women and marvels at their conduct. The
novels are less about him and more about male
stereotyping of women and about women's re-
sponses to what patriarchal society expects of them
sexually. The female characters are familiar Glasgow
types: the old-fashioned belle, the mature woman of
judgment, the stern Calvinist, the thwarted virgin,
the fallen woman, and the liberated, hard-hearted
girl.

The novels show that whatever a woman does
sexually to please a man is a mistake. Here, "the
conformist and the non-conformist to men's chival-
rous delusions about women are punished with equal
severity,"[3] observed Cabell. A woman's wisest course
is to free herself from sexual involvement and become an observer of others' predicaments. For if love
and marriage are uppermost in all minds, these pur-
suits are shown to be scarcely worth the trouble they
inspire. Glasgow's novels of manners betray a deep
distrust of physical love, which she sees as inevitably
founded in folly, vanity, and lechery. Among those
who love or think they do are the egotists, the de-
stroyers, the flighty, the deluded, and the mad. Glasgow abandons plots, never her strong point, and re-
sorts to clustering her characters and assigning them
discourses. Grouped into complementary pairs of triangles, they reflect the attitudes of their historical
periods or suffer at the mercy of fixed ideas and dimly
understood hungers.

The Romantic Comedians (1926)

Glasgow's "first comedy, *The Romantic Comedians,*
seemed to bubble out with an effortless joy."[4] Having
written with bitterness of betrayed women who

learned to live without the happiness of love, she now mocks the fatuous male who thinks polygamous happiness is his prerogative. She lets him taste humiliation when his young second wife runs off with a lover.

"This tragicomedy of a happiness-hunter"[5] centers on Judge Gamaliel Bland Honeywell, a dignified, self-deceived sexagenarian widower. He is surrounded by women who fulfill various roles, wifely, sisterly, motherly, daughterly. Their ages and characters are largely reflected through his eyes.

There is the hovering shade of his proper wife, Cordelia, who had worn herself to death caring for him. What, he now wonders, would she think of his choice of a new girl bride? He misses Cordelia on his second honeymoon. If only she were there to look after his queasy digestion. His faithful fiancée is the statuesque womanly woman of the Victorian era, fifty-eight-year-old Amanda Lightfoot. She has adored Gamaliel ever since their broken engagement thirty-seven years before. Blowsy Edmonia Bredalbane, the Judge's ugly twin, is an adventuring hedonist who has survived several husbands and lovers. She lives only to please herself and presumes to counsel her brother—to his outrage. Bella Upchurch is a widow whose keen sense of reality enables her to adjust gracefully to situations that would have scandalized her own mother. She has to be adaptable to survive. In her late forties, she would be of a suitable age for the Judge. He finds her a soothingly companionable "older" woman, but prefers her luminously lovely daughter, Annabel, whom he tenderly romanticizes as a naked woodland nymph.

Part I traces Judge Honeywell's growing infatuation with Annabel, leading to their marriage. Part II records the disillusion and collapse of the marriage within a year. The unhappy Judge resigns himself to sickness and age, only to revive when ogling the young, pretty nurse sent to care for him. Spring comes round again, for the novel ends as it began, in April love.

The personage of Judge Honeywell links *The Romantic Comedians* to Roman comedy, for the *senex amans*—the elderly lover—was a stock figure of the classical stage.[6] Once the old man persuades himself that he is ripe for love with a young girl, his punishment and suffering provide the material of merciless satire. Glasgow wreaks her vengeance on the dignified Virginia jurist,[7] vestryman, and member of the Archaelogical Society by singling out his vanity and giving him a flatteringly false perception of himself.

The Honeywell of Part I feels youthful compared to his friends. The women are all ruins, since they are said to age faster than men. The memory of his ninety-year-old father, who had sired twelve children, and the sight of plethoric gentlemen of eighty foxtrotting on spindly legs make him feel "that at sixty-five he was too young to renounce the innocent pleasures of life." Despite his confidence, and despite the twittering and budding and greening that is going on in his tempestuous heart, his person receives close, harsh scrutiny. The novelist's eye does not spare the lean stiff angularity, the brittle shanks, the veined and desiccated hands, the "mottled stains under the eyes that flowed into the sallow flush of the high cheek-bones, the corded folds of the throat." When the Judge tentatively kisses Annabel, he feels a vital surge in his "inelastic arteries." His arms of wood grasp her like dead tree branches. As he thrillingly embraces her he wonders whether his amorous behavour is in keeping with his reputation.

Honeywell's self-image as a "renowned authority in jurisprudence" allows the novelist to ring the changes on "judgment," "judicial," "masculine authority," and "law" whenever the Judge forms a thought or enunciates an opinion. He is, however, infirm of judgment, intoxicated with "the delicious aroma of youth." His recurring sexual reveries are of Annabel's unclad limbs or of

the glimmering ivory shapes of nymphs, who danced on rose-white feet to the music of running water. In spirals and wreaths and garlands, faintly coloured like the earliest spring petals, they spun round him, whirling, drifting, flying, in the wind .... Clusters of girls, curving, swaying, bending, advancing, retreating, and always they smiled as they retreated, into the iridescent mist of April.

The daydream merges with an actual ball, in which flowerlike girls whirl beguilingly over the dance floor. This social event brings out all Queenborough's gentlewomen, both debutantes and chaperones. In choosing a second wife, Honeywell feels "public opinion firmly pushing him toward the past,"[8] toward queenly Amanda. But he resists the push. While he reveres all she represents, her silent suffering, sweet patience, and reserve, she leaves him cold. He finds her presence funereal and thinks of sending her a bouquet at the same time he has flowers sent to his wife's grave.

At the ball his fantasies impel him toward the girls of twenty who are caught in the eddying dance. Throughout the novel dancing symbolizes the tumultuous and confusing changes in modern mores. Revolutions across the dance floor mean revolutions in manners, social as well as sexual. Alone, the Judge reflects that "dancing would perhaps be the best way to glide over the slippery transitional period." Now he feels a shameless longing to join the sexual dance, "with these images of fire and snow, without corsets and without conversation."

He seals his fate when he paternally, correctly,

waltzes Annabel to the other side of the room. He proposes to her, thereby deflating the long-constant Amanda and amazing Annabel's mother. But Bella suavely adjusts her temper to smile upon the match. With all her arts of flattery, her curves, and pigeonly cooings, Bella has always just scraped by. The Judge has given Annabel costly presents. Annabel is disabused of romance, for she was recently jilted. She will marry the rich old Judge so that he can pay their debts and assure the Upchurches material security.

But the honeymooning Judge Honeywell of Part II finds that continental touring, treacherous French sauces, and marriage with a girl forty-two years his junior are demanding exercise that bring on exhaustion and nervous dyspepsia. Sailing homeward, he gratefully composes his thin limbs in a deck chair, while Annabel plays and dances with the youths of her own age who think Honeywell is her father.

Annabel's dancing constitutes her chief diversion when they return to Queenborough. Too weary to accompany her, too generous to inhibit her pleasure, Honeywell hugs familiar home comforts, his knitted robe, his chair by the fire, and his thimbleful of old Bumgardner, while Annabel ceaselessly whirls in her gossamer gowns and gleaming shoes. Dancing, which had earlier seemed to hold forth a promise of youth and joy in the changing future, now reflects Annabel's apparent shallowness as well as the dizzying aimlessness that Glasgow felt characterized the new age. A vision of the lost, undone Annabel coming toward her husband with rueful mysterious beauty, torn rose-colored frock, and tumbling loosened hair, presages her fate. She falls violently in love with young Dabney Birdsong and comes home to weep night after night. She shrinks from her aging husband's caresses and sleeps in another room. A happiness hunter herself, the changed Annabel thirsts for love without postponement. Her refrain is: "If I can't have love, I'd rather die!"

Once Annabel had seemed to her husband to mirror perfection. Now her fleeting form becomes "a symbol, not only of his lost paradise but of all the burning desire of the world." He tries not to admit the truth of what he suspects, that extravagant, scatterbrained, banal Annabel is perhaps just "a normal woman."

Honeywell's earlier iridescent visions give way in the novel's second half to a series of brilliant mirrored flashes of cold truth. One night while he is sitting with the mothers and chaperones watching Annabel spinning on the dance floor "as elusive as the stars," he catches a glimpse of his face in a ballroom mirror:

. . . It seemed to him that a caged eagle gazed back at him from his bright dark eyes—a spirit, restless, craving, eternally unsatisfied, yet with a wild comedy in its despair.

When they return from the evening, Annabel, kimono slipping over ivory shoulders, smiles at him in their bedroom mirror. A bladelike chill seeps into Honeywell's heart as he thinks: "She will look like this when I am dead." On other occasions, the glass gives him back his true aging image, pale and stringy. In a final crushing vision, he beholds the mirrored reflection of his wife in her lover's arms.

At last he relinquishes his desperate clutching at happiness. Throughout *The Romantic Comedians,* all the characters descant on a happiness as fugitive and tantalizing as Annabel herself. Those who are disappointed hollowly reiterate they are perfectly happy, attempting to prolong their illusions as their malaise deepens. When, in a typical Glasgow insight, a sadder Annabel admires "all women who have learned to be happy without happiness," the Judge imagines that like all women she is "subject to moods" or "nerves." Finally acknowledging how brittle happiness is, Honeywell lets Annabel go and sadly returns to his old life.

Glasgow saves her protagonist from being merely a pompous grostesque and permits him a measure of depth. In a masterly fashion that is both delicate and harsh she delineates the tremulous minutiae of emotion, anguish, doubt, and terror he suffers while he continues to prop himself up with vain delusions. His overestimation of Annabel has been a substitute for the beauty, mystery, and sense of divinity lacking in his life. Finally he acknowledges his error and does not spare himself from scathing reproaches. Waking from his dream of false felicity, he resigns himself to the remaining comforts of age —his pipe, library, whiskey, and friends.

But as the narrative threatens to deepen into something like a morality play, with crabbed age becoming disabused of pride, lechery, and folly, Glasgow skillfully diverts the ending away from anything so lugubrious as total repentance. She allows the Judge to feel his dauntless heart grow green again at the sight of another young woman. So the ending reestablishes the cycle of human hope and error.

Bella Upchurch, in helping Judge Honeywell to overcome his gloom, at first dispenses healing blandishments and pious sentiments about the loss of respect for the sanctity of marriage. Eventually she emerges as the novel's detached moralist, composedly assessing the entire cast as a "company of happiness-hunters," "a troupe of romantic comedians." It is Bella whose acerbic pronouncements on love sound increasingly like Glasgow's own views: Everyone should experience love just "once, if only to find out how much it has been exaggerated." At home she happily surveys the blessings of her solitude. Awaiting her perusal under a redly glowing lamp, "the afternoon paper, secure from male aggression, lay still folded". "There was nothing more agitating than the tranquil immunity of a mind that had finished with love."

The circumscribed world of *The Romantic Comedians* is one of controlled artifice. Its images are flowers, dancing, jewels, light, and mirrors. The characters fall into three pairs. The lovers of the older generation are the Judge and Amanda, an appropriate couple that never gets together because of the Judge's vanity. The younger lovers caught in the sensual dance are Annabel and Dabney. In the middle generation are the two women past love, Bella and Edmonia, who look on and shrewdly comment.

Cast and chorus of this drawing-room comedy expose human frailty, offering the corrective of laughter. Illusions are finely blown away. Glasgow writes with cold aplomb in a style that is classic yet perennially fresh and entertaining. Always the moralist, she condemns obsessive happiness hunting and the shrill demand for gratification as signs of the changing times. Even more evident is the venting of female wrath that seeks gleefully to puncture and punish the vanity of the patriarchal male. But because Glasgow tempers vengeance with humor, even charity, *The Romantic Comedians* escapes from the furious overkill that mars *Barren Ground*. It remains a fine comedy, worthy of wider recognition.

They Stooped to Folly (1929)

Each ensuing Queenborough novel presents a darker vision. Begun with the intended effect of "faintly sardonic laughter," *They Stooped to Folly*

grew more serious.[9] Glasgow's title refers to Oliver
Goldsmith's verses, which she quotes:

> When lovely woman stoops to folly,
> And finds too late that men betray,
> What charm can soothe her melancholy?
> What art can wash her guilt away?[10]

She omits the poem's reply to these rhetorical quer-
ies, that the woman's only recourse "is to die." How
sexually experienced women of Glasgow's time actually did cope with public opinion and how "the feminine sense of sin" was understood in the modern
world are topics that give rise to a range of specula-
tions in this novel.

Preferring discourse to plot, Glasgow reveals her
characters through interior monologues and conver-
sational exchanges. The points of view are chiefly of
an older generation, viewing past and present mores
after World War I. Men and women are said to be
breeds apart who speak different languages. There is
no longer any accepted standard of conduct or agree-
ment as to the sexes' obligations toward each other.
With the unstable sexual morality serving as an index
to the chaos of modern times, several of the characters find themselves so disoriented as to wonder
about the meaning of life.

The novel's events cover the period from November to January, 1923 to 1924. Part I, "Mr. Littlepage," centers on that figure of Virginia gentlemanli-
ness as he reflects on the fallen women of three
generations: the sweet martyred Victorian lady,
the tarnished seductress of the early part of the century, the independent new woman of the twenties.
Also introduced are his prim wife and his beautiful
daughter, who returns with her new husband from
her tour of wartime nursing. In Part II, "Mrs. Littlepage," his wife awaits her death with calm. She and

other women characters assess their situations with respect to men. Part III, "False Spring," returns to Mr. Littlepage. He is tempted to engage in a love affair, but when his wife dies, his feelings of guilt will keep him faithful to her memory.

Virginius Littlepage of Part I is a successful lawyer of fifty-seven, portly and dignified. The war has shaken all his old complacencies. He gloomily feels that he has always observed the proprieties and that pleasure has passed him by. These philosophical reflections lead to sexual ones. About his proper wife he feels an old-fashioned pride in her "natural frigidity." Whereas he thinks of her as monogamous, his own longings cannot be satisfied in matrimony. For a decade he has daydreamed about voluptuous Amy Dalrymple with her cooing, dovelike voice. Long ago Amy had been divorced for adultery and had gone abroad. Remarried and widowed, she joined the war as an ambulance driver, saved soldiers under fire, and was decorated for heroism. Queenborough polite society still does not admit her. Now nearly fifty, she lives according to her beautiful warm-blooded whims, discreetly engaging in love when she chooses. Virginius compares her plight to those of the two other "ruined" women he knows.

His old Aunt Agatha, seduced and pregnant in the 1880s, has never recovered from her disgrace and wears out her life as a back-bedroom poor relation. Her undoer has gone unscathed. An eccentric with her furry gray shawl and bright eyes, she squirrels away sweets and gobbles banana splits at soda fountains. She likes films about sin and passion. The war has given her a new interest—sewing soldiers' pajamas. In an age that held sexuality to be a masculine diversion, any Southern lady with a taste for it was considered mentally afflicted. Agatha's mind is later revealed in a fragmented though pertinent monologue about propriety and persecution. Some of her thoughts are that fallen women, like witches and animals, are hunted for men's sport, and that "Father used to say that a woman's mind is like a flower, designed to shed fragrance, not sense."

The third unchaste woman of Virginius's acquaintance is his secretary, Milly Burden, who exemplifies "the present age with its liberal views of sin." She has borne a child, who died, but has never told her war-shocked soldier-lover. Thin, hollow-cheeked, and flat-bosomed in the new style of the 1920s, Milly appeals to Virginius's pity. Vulnerable yet tough, Milly refuses to repent and to accept the definition of female ruin. She bravely insists on her rights to live as she chooses and spoil her life in her own way. Although Virginius thinks Milly at times "unwomanly," he discerns in her a "vein of iron," inherited presumably from her unforgiving Calvinist mother, Kesiah Burden. Eventually, Milly decides against love, wanting something better.

Virginius learns that his daughter, Mary Victoria, has married the soldier who seduced Milly Burden. Now Virginius suffers moral shock at his daughter's lack of concern for Milly's stronger claim. Part I ends having established the novel's two love triangles: Virginius, his wife, and the desirable Amy form the group of elders; the soldier, Martin Welding, his wife, Mary Victoria, and abandoned Milly are the juniors. The older generation remains repressed and stabilized despite their yearnings; the young are given to acting out their desires. Self-indulgent and lacking direction, they prove no happier than their elders.

Part II explores women's viewpoints and relationships. This central, predominantly feminine section is designed to contrast with the male outlook of Part I, though Virginius is, admittedly, a wavering example of masculinity, and the other male characters are minor and sketchily drawn. Glasgow deliberately airs the women's exchanges of views, feeling that "more and more, in the modern world, women are coming to understand their interdependence as human beings." She believed that "the novelist, since he is usually a man," found certain kinds of female relationships "deficient alike in the excitement of sex and the masculine drama of action" and that these were therefore apt to be neglected in literature.[11] She shows Victoria Littlepage alone and in relation to three other women: her friend Louisa, her daughter, Mary Victoria, and Kesiah Burden, Milly's mother.

Outwardly, Victoria Littlepage is the womanly woman, trained to soothe male vanity. But she turns out to be less bland than her husband thinks and more subversive of the order both have striven to maintain. She has had her own fantasies, an imagined lover who would carry her with wild horses over the broomsedge. She guiltily regards her husband as unexciting, and she realizes that she longs for "something more satisfying than marriage."

Admitting to herself "that in her heart of hearts she had never really liked men," Victoria maintains her tenderest friendship with Louisa Goddard. An unmarried woman who prefers to be an observer of married life, Louisa has bid adieu to Victorian notions about womanly forbearance that tortured and warped female minds. Louisa has always adored Victoria. Victoria, though long married to Virginius, had not "really enjoyed him as naturally as she enjoyed Louisa, . . . [who] had understood her more absolutely than any man can understand the woman he loves." Fearing readers might infer a sapphic relationship, Glasgow points out that this was happily "before the serpent of Freudian psychology had poisoned the sinless Eden of friendship."

Confronting her selfish daughter, the radiant,

red-haired Mary Victoria, who seeks her mother's
help in reforming her new alcoholic husband, Mrs.
Littlepage feels weary of her ladylike role as a benign
influence for a better world. Dying has made Mrs.
Littlepage indifferent to doing her duty. To her,
earthly experience appears evanescent.

With Kesiah Burden, Glasgow introduces the
Calvinist obsession with sin. Kesiah's thoughts, colored by divine wrath and the blood of the lamb, stray
to her unregenerate lover, faithless husband, and un-
repentant daughter. The darker side of the betrayed
woman theme surfaces in Kesiah's consciousness, for
she recalls rumors that Agatha's illegitimate infant
had been strangled, its body found in a cinder barrel.
Kesiah's pessimistic, winding thoughts lead her to
the question that besets others—what is the meaning
of it all? When Victoria and Kesiah meet, each
woman, a pained mother aching for her daughter,
separately echoes the other's thoughts: Not for the
whole world would she live her life again.

Victoria gradually detaches herself from the
business of living and retrenches her failing energies
within herself. Mystically contained, she feels as if a
"luminous veil" enveloped her, shielding her from
sensation and obligation and releasing her from time.

Part III opens in a deceptively warm January.
Mr. Littlepage visits Amy, with whom he feels he is
"living again in a man's world"; that is, he can desire
her without respecting her. Her moist eyes, voluptuous purring, full bosom, and magnolia white hands
make his head buzz like murmuring bees. However,
he hears himself telling her she ought to take up
charity work to occupy her energy. Amy secretly,
accurately, assesses Virginius as unventuresome. His
lifelong habit of repression wins out; their meeting
ends with his escaping her with relief.

Virginius returns home to find that Victoria has

peacefully died on her couch, possibly during the hour that he has been dallying with Amy. As a widower now, filled with guilty repugnance toward Amy, he is abruptly released from the triangle in which he was caught. Martin abandons his wife, Mary Victoria, and as Milly Burden no longer wants him, the second triangle breaks apart. The conclusion leaves each character suspended in isolation. Mary Victoria, like her predecessor, Milly, awaits her baby alone. Milly leaves her mother and Queenborough to search for something better than love. Louisa and Virginius must continue without the Victoria they loved. Twilight smothers the radiance of the sunset, hinting of an uncertain future for all.

Postwar materialism and the sense of futility impelled Glasgow to single out the altered sexual morality as a sign of the new times. The men are just as polygamous as ever, as Virginius continually tells himself. But the war has had a transforming effect on women's sexuality. First, the definitions of female conduct have changed. Victorians had termed the sexually experienced woman one who had "forgotten herself"; nowadays she was one who demanded the right to live fully. Glasgow was ambivalent: She could not approve the destructive Victorian judgment that fell upon unvirginal women, nor could she countenance "the bold modern trend toward loose behaviour in love." So the novel finds satirical fault with both views, and Glasgow expands on this in her preface.

The older morality revered female chastity as a force giving solace and uplift to males, a force that stood, they said, between humanity and the jungle. Its defenders, chiefly men, were responsible for creating other crippling myths about women. The ancient overall myth is of female inferiority. There were myths that made willful, inconvenient women

into "impediments" and docile women into "inspira-
tions." So busy were women flattering men that they
could not find time to compose myths for themselves.
Many women embraced the male-created myths and
endured the martyrdom they imposed. Others, like
Victoria Littlepage, who accepted their roles as "in-
spirations," had to admit that the position was both
strenuous and unrewarding. Glasgow decided that
They Stooped to Folly would embody "one of the
immemorial woman myths," invented and sanc-
tioned by male vanity—the myth of the ruined
woman.[12]

The new morality would sensibly condemn such
myths as barbarous hypocrisies that sacrificed
women. Victoria, growing bold, observes that ruined
women are a superstition, like goblins. If you cease to
believe, they cease to exist. Amy intelligently attacks
the perpetrators of the myth. She observes that "the
sex that invented battle and murder and rape . . .
invented also, without a change of heart apparently,
monogamy and the perfect lady and the Protestant
Episcopal Church." But Amy is not permitted to be
Glasgow's ideal woman, for she is endlessly entan-
gled in a web of sensuality, preening herself only for
masculine homage. The new liberated woman, Milly,
injured by a precipitous plunge into sexuality and
thereafter cured by it, seems hysterically dominated
by two fixed ideas. Her mechanical refrain about her
rights and her insistence on happiness without an
object betray Glasgow's real feeling—that the young
are hard, shallow, and egotistical.

Since the contest between the old and the new
morality remains unresolved, the wisest course
would seem to be to remain aloof. The skeptical observers, Louisa and eventually Victoria, appear sane
in their withdrawal and their female bonding.

While skillfully able to evoke the older generation's bewilderment and weariness, Glasgow has difficulty—as she increasingly does in the mature novels—in creating younger characters. Martin, Mary Victoria, even Milly, seen through their elders' eyes, appear brittle and one dimensional. The novel's satire, occasionally sly and quirky, glimmers only fitfully, with nothing like the sustained vigor of *The Romantic Comedians.* Failing in the art of fiction, *They Stooped to Folly* engages the reader chiefly in its investigations of male and female social behavior.

The Sheltered Life (1932)

The last Queenborough novel is set earlier than the others, beginning in 1906 and ending in the autumn of 1914 just after the outbreak of the world war. The aristocrats of Queenborough, a more realistic version of Richmond than that of the two earlier novels, find themselves poised between the nineteenth and twentieth centuries. Memories go back to the brilliant balls of the 1890s when visiting dignitaries danced with reigning belles. But the city deteriorates; industry has launched an "invasion of ugliness" and has conquered. The new factory, a sign of economic advance, brings with it a pervasive chemical smell that wafts through open windows and is enough "to spoil the delicate flavour of living."

The smell symbolizes more than industrial change. The sheltering illusions, the gentle manners, the cult of beauty, the lingering romance of the old Southern gracious life—all that Glasgow meant by "evasive idealism"—are now seen to be cruel lies. They mask an undercurrent of egotism, that of the unbridled "happiness hunters," whose pursuit of sexual gratification provokes domestic catastrophe. The adulterous male, who has always seized on philander-

ing as his prerogative, is now encouraged and joined
by the sexually aware young girl of the modern generation. Glasgow sees the decline of morality, the
deterioration of the city and of the region, and the
imminent global war all as aspects of one downward
movement.

Three generations coexist just after the turn of
the century. Jenny Blair Archbald is a charming, vital
girl of nine with a propensity for pleasure. Her
grandfather, General David Archbald, is a civilized
man with the impulses of a poet, who at seventy-five
has memories of slavery and the Civil War. In the
middle generation is their lovely neighbor, Eva Birdsong, once a famous belle of the 1890s. She endures
and ignores the infidelities of her handsome husband, George, throughout the twelve years of their
marriage. At the last discovering him in the embrace
of the now grown Jenny Blair, she shoots and kills
him with his hunting rifle. The chief observers and
reflectors of what happens are the old General and
his granddaughter, Jenny Blair, both of whom in
their separate ways adore Eva for her beauty.

In Part First, "The Age of Make-Believe," Jenny
Blair lives in a household of downtrodden female
relatives over which her grandfather presides. Jenny
Blair's precocity is evident in her craving for adventure and her little narcissistic song: "I'm alive, alive,
alive, and I'm Jenny Blair Archbald."

Living nearby are George and Eva Birdsong. In
her thirties, bronze-haired Eva Birdsong is still rav-
ishing, with eyes like flying bluebirds. The quality of
her beauty is almost an abstract ideal to be wor-
shipped and recounted in stories. It has been known
to stop processions and is still spoken of as "allegory"
and "legend." For Eva this reputation is, of course,
a crushing burden, as she later acknowledges, for
human beauty must inevitably succumb to the

ravager time. She is occasionally seen to droop and look faint when she thinks she is unobserved. As her beauty is all she has, however, she disciplines herself to maintain it. Her conversation reveals an obsession with old triumphs of bygone waltzes. Having sacrificed a musical career to marry her improvident young lawyer husband, she must maintain the fiction that theirs is a blissfully perfect marriage. While her husband philanders, Eva props herself up on her illusions. "The code of perfect behaviour supported her as firmly as if it had been a cross." Economies require her to do her own housework; she neglects her garden, which runs to ruin and foreshadows her own fate.

The child Jenny Blair engages in a secret flirtation with George, its thrill intensified by her discovery of him with his handsome black mistress. She also adores Eva, whom she helps remake an old 'nineties ball gown for a party. Eva confides her deluded philosophy to the girl, "that a great love doesn't leave room for anything else in a woman's life." They speak of her early hopes to be a great singer, "but that was before I fell in love. After that, I stopped wanting anything else."

The dancing party climaxes the first part. The vision of George and Eva waltzing together fulfills every spectator's romantic dreams. But when George wanders off into the moonlit garden with one of the pretty young girls, Eva's poise is shattered. Convulsed with anguish, her primrose satin gown crushed, she hurls herself on a bedroom couch and gives vent to the most luxuriant grief. Awed, Jenny Blair and the other children go on tip-toe at this sight of the adult world with its illusion of fairyland perfection torn down. George is sent for and comes to gather up his wife. Jenny Blair closely observes Eva's extreme joy and transfiguration: "She gave herself to his arms as if she were yielding up more than her body." Jenny Blair yields to her own feeling of ecstasy:

Without and within, she felt the rain of delight, sprinkling her body and soul, trickling over her bare flesh, seeping down through her skin into the secret depths of her heart.

Once again she sings her narcissistic song.

Part Second, "The Deep Past," takes place eight years later in the consciousness of General Archbald. Eva is in the hospital undergoing a maiming female operation. Archbald, who is devoted to her, pities her; he nevertheless defends her husband's infidelities in the language of a sexual double standard: "All that side of his life has no more to do with his devotion to Eva than if—than if it were malaria from the bite of a mosquito." On the differences between men and women, he feels that "life would be more agreeable if women could realize that man is not a monogamous animal."

He reflects on his own disappointed hopes, of being a poet, of marrying a woman he had loved. Instead he conformed to the conventional expectations of others. He sees his life as the playing of correct roles: "He had been, indeed, everything but himself. Always he had fallen into the right pattern; but the centre of the pattern was missing." An observer between two worlds, Archbald exudes a gentle pessimism with respect to humanity's future.

Part Third, "The Illusion," opens with General Archbald's emerging from his reveries and catching sight of budding Jenny Blair, the embodiment of the future. Her "captive impulses" seem to cry "Let me out! Let me out!" Nearly eighteen, Jenny is being prepared by her mother for a début; instead she would like to get away from Queenborough and go to New York, perhaps to be an actress or a suffragette. "I don't care about men," she exclaims, and like other young Queenborough women, "All I want to do is to live my own life."

In contrast to the new, energetic Jenny Blair, Eva Birdsong still lies passively in the hospital for her operation. Even as she awaits the surgeon's knife, Eva continues to maintain her faith in love and to excuse her husband's philandering as "kindness." It becomes clear that she does not want to live. "What she feared most was not death, but life with its endless fatigue, its exacting pretense."

Jenny Blair is torn between her hysterical anxiety over Eva and her wakened sensuality and guilty crush on Eva's husband. She decides to give Eva her own blue nightgown and her new Japanese silk kimono with its purple wistaria vine twisting upon a blue sky. "She longed to sacrifice herself for Mrs. Birdsong." Despite this superficial sorrow for Eva, she is flooded with joy at finding herself alone with George. She entices him to stolen kisses. Surely, she thinks, it cannot harm Eva for her to cherish this secret love deep within her heart, this "flowing tide of sensation." She hopes for happiness, but passes a night of fearful dreaming, of running in circles through a dark wood from an unseen pursuer.

The operation destroys Eva's beauty. This loss of her identity at forty shatters her. She suffers a postoperative "nervous breakdown" and behaves erratically, breaking into panic, weeping wildly, wandering off alone. She cannot keep up the pretenses of her old life. But she continues to have moments of clear understanding of her plight: "When you've never been yourself for forty years, you've forgotten what you really are." With Jenny Blair, she becomes candid and offers counsel. Admitting the truth of what her own life has been, she tries to warn Jenny Blair against staking everything on a single chance for

love: "Always keep something back, if it is only a
crumb. Always keep something back for a rainy day."
Giving up all for love is to become "a slave to fear":

"Fear of losing love. Fear of losing the power that won love
so easily. I sometimes think there is nothing so terrible for
a woman . . . as to be loved for her beauty."

Despite these lucid moments, Eva is to sink into a
deeper void of terror and madness. She goes away to
recuperate and her garden decays apace.

   In her absence Jenny Blair and George meet at
intervals for ecstatic embraces. One day Jenny finds
George, the eager sportsman, at home with the wild
ducks he has shot. The wantonness of their slaughter
emphasizes George's enjoyment of killing living
creatures as he has helped destroy his wife.

Dead feathers! But he liked them dead. He was never so
happy, she knew, as when he had just killed something
beautiful. . . . He appeared to be perfectly happy. He was
not troubled by love; he was not troubled by self-reproach.

Jenny Blair and George embrace in the library, supposing Eva to be upstairs in her room. They are fro-
zen by the apparition of Eva. Jenny Blair runs into
the garden, where she crouches in the shadows and
then runs animal-like in frenzied circles, as in her old
dream. The reports of the hunting gun mingle with
street noises. The evil smell curls up from the factory
below. "Nothing has really happened," Jenny Blair
tells herself.

   George lies dead in his chair with lips bloodied
like the beaks of the scattered birds. Eva sits rigidly
staring into the twilight, her face like a skull. We can
only infer that at this moment, stripped of illusion,
she confronts at last her rage at her ruined life. A
nephew of hers and General Archbald appear as if
from nowhere, taking control, asserting that "an ac-

cident," has happened, exonerating Eva as well as
Jenny Blair. Jenny Blair cries out, as her grandfather
encloses her innocence in his sheltering arms, "I
didn't mean anything in the world."

The irony of the closure is that none of the characters is allowed to assess the significance of what
happens. It is this that makes the work a dark satire
rather than a tragedy. Violent events bring no com-
pensatory vision. The males in authority judge these
events as unintentional and the women as innocent.
Jenny Blair denies that anything has happened or
that anything was meant. Eva's secret thoughts are
locked from the reader. The sheltered life can go on
as before. Just as it shielded Jenny Blair from moral
responsibility in her demands for gratification, so it
will shield Eva from any disagreeable encounters
with the law. Powerful kin close protectively around
the guilty.[13]

The "evasive idealism" that Glasgow thought in-
fected Southern culture is still operative. It falsifies
the most predatory impulses and gratuitous suffering
under the name of beautiful behavior. George is said
to be kind, the Birdsong marriage perfect, Jenny Blair
a romantic innocent, Eva beautiful. Eva Birdsong
becomes a powerful symbol of the perverse insistence
on keeping up appearances in the teeth of reality. Yet
others in her world accept her beauty as a positive
good, even as a moral and heroic force. The truth
about her and her marriage has deterred no one from
worshipping the appearance of her perfection.

To each person in the novel Eva means something. She attracts different kinds of worship from
her adorers. Her husband may love her, but he finds
her perfection unendurable:

"I know I'm not a big man, and when I come up against
anything that is too much for me, beauty, goodness, unhap-

piness, I give way inside. I can't stand but so much of a thing, and then I break up, and that's all there is of me. When that happens, I am obliged to get out of it. Any-where."

The General in his poet's heart worships her as an historically and aesthetically potent object. She is like the humiliated South, for in her face he sees the defeat that he "saw in many faces after the war." His view of her is elegiac. The passing of her beauty is "the decay of the age, a part of the lost sense of glory." He believes finally that "life would never again melt and mingle into the radiance that was Eva Birdsong." Jenny Blair, too, perceives something of this:

What Mrs. Birdsong meant to her, she felt vaguely, was order, beauty, perfection, an unattainable ideal of living.

To see her changed, stricken, defeated by life, with her glory dragged in the dust, was too terrible.

But for Jenny Blair as a member of the same sex, Eva is also a model, someone she may emulate, someone she may become. Not so regally splendid as Eva, Jenny Blair can take the short route to displacing her. In the arms of Eva's husband, whom she incestuously sees as fatherly, she can receive a fragment of the same sexual homage he accords Eva. And she can clothe Eva in her own nightgown and robe, by this means merging her identity with Eva's without the awful burden of becoming a legend or an allegory.

Between Eva and Jenny Blair is played out the old conflict that absorbed Glasgow from the begin-ning of her career—the conflict between civilization and biology. Eva's carefully wrought, rigorously sus-tained beauty is, like her long suppression of her true feelings, the result of culture. But driving through Jenny Blair are inherent needs emerging as forces that are both genetic and primordial. Her family history has included erratic and tempestuous personalities, even alleged witches. More powerful, more ancient, is the atavistic life force, the sexual vitality that has "swept her away in its claws" and that she does not resist. It is the force that drives and torments her like a hunted animal in dream and in actuality, absolving her of responsibility:

Millions of years before she was born, it must have lain somewhere, that hunger, waiting, wanting, as dumb as the earth or the rocks. Millions of years, and now it came to life and sprang out at her. All the waiting, the wanting, of millions of years! She was too young to bear all that weight, the weight of earth and rocks for millions of years. . . . "It isn't my fault," she said aloud to the mirror."

The Sheltered Life composes yet another variation on the theme of evolution. "Alive" Jenny Blair is the egotistical survivor, willing to assert her sexual energy and to shunt others aside. Glasgow saw this as a deplorable quality of the hard-hearted young, and she would display increasing intolerance of the newer generation. Jenny Blair is able to have it both ways. Even as she allows herself to yield to the demands of "biology," she can take privileged refuge in the lies and evasions offered by "civilization," without ever confronting the consequences of her actions.

The novel's three generations—the General, the Birdsongs, and Jenny Blair—are paired off into the sacrificed idealists who subscribe to an older morality (Eva and the General), and the destructive happiness hunters of the new dispensation (Jenny Blair and George). Darwinian notions of defeat and survival as they apply to the old and new South are superimposed upon each pair. But characteristically, Glasgow is intent upon exploring Eva and Jenny Blair as

women as well as symbols. She makes her usual indictment against sexual love, male homage, female
sacrifice. But she is unable to escape from her own
ambivalence as to how a woman should deal with her
sexuality. Her sympathy, even love, are clearly for
the older woman. Yet while she deplores her sacrifice, she admires and idealizes the martyred product. She grants her the right to slay her husband, but
to judge from the noncommittal ending, Eva has had
to destroy herself as well. If Glasgow feels the ex-
ploited Eva requires pity, she forces the younger,
freer woman to excite animosity. Jenny Blair, the
independent girl who accepts her sexuality, who rejects the role of the Southern *débutante*, who wants
to do something with her life (Glasgow disdainfully
lumps suffragette with actress), is made to pursue a
shallow, treacherous course. Ultimately, Glasgow is
signalling the dangers for women, whether liberated
or not, of locating their identities in their sexuality.

The critical fortunes of *The Sheltered Life* de-
serve notice. It was immensely praised by critics and
accorded front page reviews in leading newspapers.
It was fully expected to win for its author a Pulitzer
Prize. There was a chance of its being made into a
play. When the prize unaccountably went to another
novel, letters and telegrams of protest and commis-
eration flooded from all quarters. Despite this failure,
which greatly embittered Glasgow, the novel remains among her distinguished works. Stylistically
elegant, *The Sheltered Life* plays off moral responsibility against the pressures of biology, and warns with
dramatic clarity of the high social and psychic cost of
illusion.

○○○○○○○○○○○○○○○○○○○○○○○○○○○○○○○

8

Virginia Between Two World Wars:
Vein of Iron (1935),
In This Our Life (1941),
Beyond Defeat (1966)

After her vigorous "excursion into civilized comedy,"[1] as Glasgow described the Queenborough novels, she abandoned that mode. Her health was deteri-
orating. In these last years of her life, she saw the
world as a baffling place. World War I, the Depression, the spectre of another major war, and what she
considered the weakening moral fiber of America
forced upon her the idea of an ever-worsening future. No longer did she care to embrace the uncer-
tainties of contemporary life within her ironic vision.
Whereas the Queenborough novels had satirically
transfixed the sexual foibles of the day, the last novels
revert to Glasgow's more characteristic view that sex
is a serious matter leading usually to disaster. These
novels reflect her growing conviction that freer sexual conduct could best be understood within a larger
context of moral dissoluteness—in honesty, altruism,
generosity, in human relationships generally.

The novels appearing from 1935 and thereafter
betray a diminution of hope, energy, talent, and literary merit. Glasgow seeks with varying persuasive-
ness to reaffirm old values, the most reliable she
knew, and to extract from them some rule for living
in a world grown rife with materialism. *Vein of Iron*
begins positively, emphasizing the strength of ancestry and an identification with the Virginia country-

side. Glasgow felt optimistic while working on it. But the last section loses the fine control of the beginning. The tone grows despairing as the novel lengthily condemns modern urban life. Manners and literature, fast cars and slang, street noise, painted women, and of course the greedy hunt for happiness are irritably and indiscriminately classed together as signs of what is wrong with America. The heroine's final praise of a life without joy fails to be convincing. *In This Our Life* produces an elderly antihero and his daughter. Both are idealists who have been beaten down in various ways; each in a gesture of defiance strikes back at a family grown morally obtuse. *Beyond Defeat*, the sequel Glasgow decided not to publish, was brought out posthumously. She had written it to counteract the critical view that *In This Our Life* was a pessimistic work. The sequel reveals the mind of an author who has already withdrawn emotionally from the bitterness of living. *Beyond Defeat* is a visionary attempt to reconstitute the benevolent family devoted to love and labor in harmony with nature.

Vein of Iron (1935)

This novel documents the passing of a sterner epoch, that of the country people from whom the Glasgows descended. The author explores family memory, reaching back to the pioneers of Rockbridge County in the Valley of Virginia where her ancestors had settled in the eighteenth century. Her heroine's parents are like her own—the delicately bred mother, the Scotch-Irish father.

    Drawing on the fortitude she connected with her father's people, Glasgow entitled the novel with her favorite phrase. She "wished . . . to test the resistance of this vein of iron to outward pressure, and to measure the exact degree of its strength."[2] The vein of iron was a feature of Calvinism. She could quarrel with Calvinism's religious teachings, but she saw that its principles could be translated into rules of conduct. In its largest sense, the vein of iron was "the vital principle of survival, which has enabled races and individuals to withstand the destructive forces of nature and of civilization."[3]

Covering the years 1901 to 1933, *Vein of Iron* takes its main characters from Ironside village to the city of Queenborough and back.

The novel's beginning creates a strong sense of place. Ironside is a tucked-away village in the Valley of Virginia where the mountains seem living presences. Fincastle ancestry is embedded in these hills, from the first scholar-pioneer. The family's ruggedness is both iron and earthlike. Family memories include legends of Indians, whose wildness provides a subtheme running through the narrative. Invoking the popular American "Indian captivity" genre, Glasgow tells of a Fincastle ancestress, Martha Tod, kidnapped and married to a Shawnee brave. Though returned, she never lost her bond with the wilderness and had spells of listening to the forest. This same wilderness spirit occasionally infects the present generations.

The Fincastle family arrangement is as patriarchal as those in the Queenborough novels, both resembling the author's home life if we recall old Francis Glasgow among his womenfolk. Family and money responsibilities burden John Fincastle. He is a clergyman-philosopher who has lost his congregation and church for his own free-thinking. Though his writing earns him distant renown, his countrymen ignore him. His daughter, Ada, is the heroine.

Each character in Part I engages in an interior

monologue, a reverie that dissolves time and space and contributes to the web of family lore. Ada's thoughts are dire. She reflects on a child's game of judge and jury that she plays, in which she is always on trial for her life. Hearing a mouse running about the dark house, she realizes it is doomed to be trapped. She wonders at God's allowing this cruel suffering of creatures, since Grandmother says the Lord "made mice to be caught in traps." Entrapment is one of the novel's main themes. The mouse's certain fate is the child's way of perceiving the Calvinist doctrine of predestination. God elects some to be saved and damns others. Related to the theme of preordained entrapment and suffering is that of mental illness. Ada's thoughts wander to the idiot boy, Toby Waters, who lives in a pigsty. Chased by other children, he suffers like an animal. "Why did God make idiots? It seemed worse than making mice to be caught in traps." The sudden squeak of the trapped mouse pierces through Ada's sleepy questioning thoughts.

Part II covers six years. Ada at twenty is engaged to Ralph McBride. With all her summer happiness and budding sensuality, Ada shares in the old family sense of humanity's hard lot. Russet-haired Ralph has a weakened will owing to the domination of his grim Calvinist mother. Forced to marry Janet, a girl who falsely accuses him of seducing her, Ralph abandons his plans to study law and turns to selling automobiles. He repeatedly laments: "I am trapped."

Jilted, Ada begins sympathetically to identify with hunted creatures and mad Toby, feeling herself to be painfully pursued. She observes a hawk seize a bird and feels the same claws at her heart. But when frivolous Janet leaves Ralph, Ada reaches for happiness by agreeing to spend three days with Ralph in a mountain hunting cabin. Thus she fulfills her dream of being with him "somewhere in the Indian trail," even "if she paid for it with all the rest of her life."

In Part III Ralph and Ada consummate their love. They seek out the old Indian Trail. Ralph offers her an Indian couch of boughs. It seems at first to Ada "that the pulse of wildness in her heart was at rest." But her joy is dimmed by puritan guilt and a sense of mutability. Indeed, the two are never again to recover their fleeting ecstasy. Ralph leaves for the war in France.

Part IV brings the expected retribution. Pregnant, Ada endures the stony reproach of her humiliated grandmother. She cannot repent, nor can she inform Ralph, who is overseas, of her pregnancy, fearing that he lacks the strength to endure the news. As an unmarried mother, Ada is pelted with mud and taunted by howling children. The incident fulfills her earlier premonitions of identification with the idiot Toby and suffering creatures.

Part V sees the Fincastles in a rundown neighborhood in Queenborough. It is 1918. Ada works as a saleswoman to support her son, Ranny. Ralph is expected any day, but his letters reveal a burnt-out weariness that bodes ill for future happiness:

"I've been living for a thousand years, and I'm as dry as a husk. And God knows I'm sick of women—except you. But you aren't a woman. You're Ada, and that's different. . . . I'm sick of women, and God knows I'm sick of mud."

They marry when he returns, but do not recover their former hopefulness. Misfortunes multiply. Ralph takes up drinking and philandering. He suffers a car accident. With the Depression he gets work in a filling station and repair shop. He grumbles about Ada's job, thinking it deprives him of his manliness. Ada relies on her inherent fortitude and cultivates a martyred sweetness. Happiness now means that each day, drained of energy, with aching, swollen feet, she will work to help Ralph and Ranny; it's "not a bit like the feeling I used to call happiness."

The Fincastles abandon Queenborough and return to the country. Alone, John goes to Ironside to die, to save funeral costs. On the homeward bus he hears the mingling babel of voices chorusing of the future: bargains, permanent waves, corn liquor, Virginia tourism, the inevitable redirection of Southern class hatred into a conflict between blacks and whites, the need for "a President that makes people happy," the boredom with private virtue and public reform, and how women nowadays can take care of themselves. John finds the ruined old homestead. The confused modern voices give way to his dying reveries of the vanished past, of his strong mother, his wife, the inhabitants of the mountains.

Ada, Ranny, and Ralph follow to build a new life in Ironside. Ada sees the changed quality of her married love, the loss of passion, as symptomatic of the "flaw . . . inherent in the very structure of living." Despite their lack of joy, she decides that all is for the best: "Never, not even when we were young, she thought, with a sudden glow of surprise, was it so perfect as this."

Glasgow believed that the inherent vein of iron would enable strong folk to resist the destructive evils of both civilization and nature. Contemporary civilization, she felt, offered only senseless change, which the young mistook for progress. Neither humanity nor the quality of life had really improved. Ada reiterates the author's despair:

She knew that life had lost a sense of permanence, of continuing tradition. What does it all mean? she thought, dazed with weariness.

John sees humanity as "still savage," civilization being "perhaps a higher level of barbarism." The author inveighs against American culture in the 1920s and 1930s, especially the effects of the "after-the-war boom." In fact, Virginia's economy suffered less in the Depression years than the rest of the nation, but Glasgow resentfully saw only rampant vulgarity. Prosperity and immorality went together. Black and white workers alike put their high wages into lace curtains, pianolas, and refrigerators. Children played gangster. Young people embraced in parked cars. Girls were wilder even than boys; "all alike" they painted their lips, pasted curls to their cheeks, tottered on little high heels. Colored maids in boarding houses bought silk stockings on installment while solid people wore serviceable cotton. Even the mountaineers had radios. America was a "strange country with its watered psychology, its vermin-infested fiction, and its sloppy minds that spill over. What hope is there for civilization as long as the lowest common denominator is the popular hero?" Only the Fincastles and a handful of hardy friends stand fast against encroaching barbarism.

Deploring World War I, Glasgow assails those Christians who, like the local minister, had taken a fierce pleasure in abetting "righteous war." She allows Mrs. McBride to represent Ironside's most fanatical type of Calvinism. Mrs. McBride had "found a thrill of cruelty in the Christian symbols of crucifixion and atonement." She was glad to be able to give a son to the cause, as she had been willing to see him suffer in his forced marriage. Ada finds that Mrs. McBride's "piety, like her patriotism, was rooted in hatred." Instead of being a civilizing force, the Calvinist spirit at its worst runs counter to the spirit of Christian love. It justifies the suffering of creatures. It has ground down Ralph's spirit. In these respects it represents for Glasgow the "still savage" aspect of civilization. The harm of the inexorable Calvinist viewpoint might be traced even in those earliest settlers who, as Ralph mutters, "set out to despoil the wilderness, defraud the Indians of their hunting-grounds, and start to build a new Jerusalem for predestinarians."

Nature is a force as powerful as civilization. The Indian and wilderness themes in *Vein of Iron* represent nature sometimes in a positive and sometimes in a negative sense. "Wild" Ada romanticizes the wilderness, which she connects with freedom and happiness. She dreams of following the Indian trail with her lover. Thoughts of joy shoot through her "with an arrowy swiftness." She yearns for fulfillment in the mountain forest where Martha Tod's ghostly Indian brave was said still to roam. Ada thinks of giving birth like an Indian "on a bed of pine boughs." She resembles that Martha, who had leaped up at the call of owl or fox and who listened to the forest.

The wilderness also means peacefulness and permanence. The living presences of the mountains infuse the Fincastles with their rocklike strength. The wilderness had created the power of endurance in those settlers who had had to survive in it. John feels a kinship with that first pioneer who founded his church here when at night his own solitary nature "slips back into the wilderness." When, weary in the city, Ada thinks nostalgically, "There must be room somewhere . . . for quiet people who wanted to live apart from the delirium of an ailing world," she implies a return to these mountains.

On the other hand, the wilderness in some instances becomes a metaphor for the violence and cruelty of the world and the conditions of life for which one must have the vein of iron to survive. The novel's imagery compares humans disadvantageously to animals—grasshoppers, pigs, mice, and hunted birds and furred creatures. Ada fears "something always waiting to pounce." The actual mountain wilderness might offer romantic Indian dreams of freedom, but it also harbored hostile savages long ago. Ada recalls a legend of the pioneer woman who saw Shawnees murder her infant, its blood and brains spattering her skirts. She survived on berries and tree bark. Martha Tod, too, survived; she did not become a savage, for during her captivity she held on to her cameo brooch, a symbol, as Glasgow hastens to explain.

When Ralph receives a head injury in a car crash, Ada dreams fearfully of being hunted by a tomahawk-wielding Shawnee, her dream linking modern civilization with savagery. Tomahawk war has simply been replaced by World War and senselessly destructive machinery. But when the dream Indian melts into a peaceful pastoral scene, the message becomes clear: They must return to the country.

Resisting the barbarism of contemporary civilization is the problem that besets the Fincastles, perhaps the South itself, as resisting savagery and surviving the natural wilderness had challenged the pioneers. The solution now is to be found in the lessons of the past, in the wisdom of ancestors. For Ada it is their legacy of fortitude:

They had come to life there in the past; they were lending her their fortitude; they were reaching out to her in adversity. This was the heritage they had left. She could lean back on their strength; she could recover that lost certainty of a continuing tradition.

For John, books and learning have dictated his solitary, visionary life course. Poor, rejected, virtually unread, he relies on an inner life sustained by the past's legacy of scholarship. His is an enlightened

form of Presbyterianism, in contrast to the hellfire
Calvinists. His beliefs are infused with mystical philosophy from several sources, Hindu, Roman, and
German. Glasgow means him to sound humane and
rational. Unfortunately for the novel, John—like Ada
and the others—tends to be an embodiment of ideas
rather than a convincing human being. His philosophy seems tentative. He flounders, unable to judge
events; for him the times are "without a pattern,
without a code, without even a center." Too sensitive, he indulges in self-pity and moral aloofness as he
surveys the world of morons and idiots, for so he sees
the "mass consciousness." He considers wretched humanity from afar, patronizingly wondering if
Negroes perhaps suffer less than other humans "or
perhaps they had learned how to suffer." As the
novel's so-called intellectual, he proves thin and
disappointing. Ada, the other moral voice, primly
and invidiously deplores the way of the world to the
extent that her assessments do not seem reliable to
the reader. At the same time, there is a soap-opera
quality in her reflections on the "something missing
in her marriage." When Ralph kisses her "she looked
in vain for the romantic gleam in his eyes." Ada is not
persuasive when she insists that life is better than
ever without love. But her gloating assertion that she
as a woman is strong while her man is weakly dependent represents an idea to which Glasgow was committed.

Despite its brave beginning that celebrates the
country people and their history, *Vein of Iron* deteriorates progressively into clichés and the excessively
long complaint of the final section. The book's tor-
rent of condemnation is unrelieved by irony.[4] It betrays Glasgow's declining health and creative powers
and her discouragement at living in a world she
could not understand and which she felt did not ap-

preciate her work. *Vein of Iron* signals Glasgow's definitive retreat before modernism, her inability to confront change that did not conform to her idea of progress, to comprehend alienation as a condition of contemporary life, or to grapple with the requirement of renewed self-definition in the fictional context of a dislocated world. Scarred and grim, her people denounce the moderns and withdraw into a haven of inherited wisdom.

In This Our Life (1941)

Glasgow did not expect to write another novel and had even felt upon completing *Vein of Iron* that her "inner springs were drained, and had run dry."[5] But on the eve of another World War she began a work for which she had but meager strength left. *In This Our Life* would round out and conclude her Virginia social history, which extended from the Civil War to 1939. She meant it to be "an analysis in fiction of the modern temper," which in the community around her she saw as "confused, vacillating, uncertain, and distracted from permanent values."[6] Heedless of the impending war, the main characters care only for their immediate happiness.[7]

The novel examines three related Queenborough families, the upper-class Timberlakes and Fitzroys, and the Clays, descended from slaves. Glasgow censures the breakdown in human ties among the upper-class family members and between the whites and the blacks, who are bound together by ancestral blood. She saw the general "weakening of the moral fibre" giving rise to greed, selfishness, hypocrisy, and betrayal, and eventually infecting the entire culture of America with vulgar materialism. As the novel's opening street scene shows, progress means demolishing a white-columned mansion to put in a gas station.

The events cover a little over a year, from April, 1938, to August, 1939, just before World War II. The Timberlakes have fallen on hard times, caught between their past pretensions of wealth and status and the present reality of limited means, illness, and family strife. As an elderly, antiheroic type, Asa Timberlake represents the last of Glasgow's civilized men with any sense of an aristocratic heritage. A menial in a tobacco factory, he feels at fifty-eight "as insecure . . . as a drying leaf on a stem." His father, a former tobacco magnate, was a suicide.

Now an enfeebled patriarch, Asa waits on his unloving wife, Lavinia, a willful hypochondriac who rules from her couch. He would prefer to be with the woman he loves, vigorous Kate Oliver. On Sundays he visits her farm, Hunter's Fare, where wholesome pleasures contrast with the morally skewed atmosphere of family life at Queenborough.

The Timberlake daughters are Roy and Stanley. Roy, according to her father, has "some hard fine grain of integrity . . . [and] . . . all the qualities . . . that men have missed and wanted in women: courage, truthfulness, a tolerant sense of humor, loyalty to impersonal ends." With her blunt, pleasant face, she is less beautiful than her spoiled younger sister. Golden-skinned, amber-haired Stanley has a pouting allure. Sheltered by her upper-class family because of her loveliness, she has learned to be selfish and deficient in moral sensitivity. Stanley represents the way Glasgow saw the new Southern girl who inherited the evasive idealism of her Victorian forebears but not their self-restraint: soft and winsome but unfeeling, willing to exploit her sexual attractiveness for personal ends. The family believes she will "always find some man to take care of her."

Stanley enjoys the special favor of her mother's rich, lecherous old uncle, William Fitzroy. He gives Stanley presents in return for her flirtatious flattery. Asa hopes old Fitzroy will bequeath money to Lavinia so that he can leave his wife for Kate.

Close to both families are the respectable Clays, former slaves who share in Fitzroy and Timberlake blood. Young Parry is an intelligent, courteous youth. In the north he would be light enough to pass for white. He wants to become a lawyer. When he looks to the Fitzroys and Timberlakes for financial help, Fitzroy tells him blacks don't need lawyers as they can always count on their white friends. Instead he gives Parry a chauffeur's job. The whites' ambivalence and hypocrisy are important ingredients in the plot.

Each of the Timberlake daughters has her man. Roy passionately adores her red-haired surgeon husband, Peter Kingsmill. A modern pair, they have accorded each other "freedom" in marriage. Stanley's fiancé is Craig Fleming. Dark and intense, he is an idealist who wants to make the world more decent. But unsure of where to place his commitment, he flits from one ideology to another. Now a kind of radical lawyer, he is restlessly in quest of causes.

Stanley covets her sister's husband, who becomes infatuated with her, and the two go away together just before Stanley and Craig were to have married. Craig reacts by drinking heavily. The betrayed Roy is left to manage her anguish. She also befriends Craig. His dependence upon her strength becomes a bond between them.

Meanwhile Peter and Stanley have stormy quarrels. Stanley spends money beyond their means, aborts her child, and goes out with other men. Unable to cope with his debts, his personal life, his work, and his drinking, Peter commits suicide. Stanley falls apart emotionally. The family brings her home to Queenborough and surround her protectively.

Four months after Peter's funeral, a restless Stanley wearies of grieving. There is a generalized malaise as the war in Europe threatens, Hitler is expected to invade Poland, young men are going to Spain. Bitterly self-engrossed, Stanley takes long wild drives alone. One night she kills a child in a hit-and-run accident. With characteristic irresponsibility, Stanley abandons her car in the black district to make it appear that Parry Clay has been driving it. Parry is arrested.

Timberlakes and Fitzroys are fully prepared to shelter Stanley and to allow Parry to be wrongly prosecuted. Fitzroy will pay for his legal counsel. Even the idealist Craig, who had promised to send Parry to Howard University, agrees now to betray him out of chivalry to Stanley. Fitzroy's wife sums it up, murmuring: "Colored people don't feel things the way we do . . . not as a young girl would, anyway. . . . " Asa confronts the family alone, summoning all his moral strength and outraged sense of honor as he demands that his daughter be turned in.

When Roy perceives how Craig has felt himself weakly drawn to her weeping sister, her disillusion is complete. No longer able to pretend love for her sister, hating Craig's defection, Roy determines to leave her home. Proud and desolate, she rushes into the rainy night. She picks up an English youth, who, she learns, is off to the war and probable death. She spends the night with him as a symbolic violation of her genteel traditions. It is her way of stepping into a new age and a new life, according to Glasgow, and of assuaging her grief and anger. She returns home the next day only briefly to collect her things and bid farewell to her father. She flings out her parting words to him: "I want something to hold by! I want something good!"[8]

The characters fall into two groups. There are the arrogant self-seekers who want to maintain their immunity as members of an established social order. And there are the others, idealists who represent forces for change. The chief supporters of the old order are Lavinia, Uncle Fitzroy, and Stanley, whom her elders have spoiled by nurturing in her their own selfish and destructive impulses. All three cling to the decaying aristocracy's sheltered life and represent the static condition of the evasive idealists.

Those who variously seek outlets for change are Kate, Parry Clay, Craig, and Roy. Their effectiveness, however, is diffused. Free, unfashionable Kate, who goes her own country way, is almost an offstage character. Parry, the "new negro" with his seemingly doomed aspirations, is a slight though sympathetic figure. Craig is an unfocused idealist who swerves in a crisis. Roy is the only character in whom Glasgow sees hope for the future:

Hers is that special aspect of youth—yesterday, today, and tomorrow—with which I have always felt most sympathetic: that youth of the adventurous heart, of the everlasting search for perfection, of the brave impulse to hazard everything upon the first, or upon the last, chance of happiness.[9]

Roy's reckless show of strength when she runs out into the night, determined to strike a blow against respectability, is one for which she will pay, as do all heroines who indulge in lovemaking just once, for whatever reason. Although Glasgow insisted that Roy's one-night stand with a stranger signifies affirmation, it has all the makings of a self-destructive act. Indeed, its fulfillment in the sequel,

Beyond Defeat—not published until twenty-one years after Glasgow's death—is Roy's pregnancy and three years of hardship, poverty, sickness, and loneliness with her illegitimate child, before returning to Queenborough.

But Glasgow pinned high hopes on Roy. In her view, young motherhood had a certain appeal. It was, after all, an affirmation of womanliness. Yet what could be more inconvenient than the necessary lover or husband who, after engaging a woman's emotions, would inevitably cause her terrible suffering? Roy's great act is to flout everything: sexual love, family bonding, masculine control, patriarchy. The child she conceives impersonally she will have to herself, so retaining her femininity and her independence. But Glasgow isn't able to save her heroine from paying a huge price for these privileges.

Between the old order and the new stands Asa, at home in neither. He sees through the family hypocrisy. For thirty years he has done what he hated for the sake of tradition. But the young, even Roy whom he loves, seem unstable and disorderly. He cannot share in their world either. The ultimate gesture of this self-effacing man in rescuing the young black shows him able to salvage the best of the old patrician sense of honor that has so deteriorated in the others. His plan to leave his wife, however, once she is financially secure, indicates his willingness to defy the past when it means the hypocrisy of a bad marriage.

But Asa is also a major flaw of the novel. Although his climactic gesture is properly heroic and credible, altogether too much of the novel's space is devoted to him in which he merely complains. Since Glasgow accords Asa an important position as a nonparticipating commentator upon events, the reader expects his perceptions to be illuminating. This expectation is disappointed. First, he is incapable of any truly ironic view of himself. For much of the novel he breathes forth an air of nerveless impotence, dejection, and self-pity, thus creating an impression of unreliability. Second, he is an insensitive observer of what happens to the rest of the family. The action centers on the switching of the two pairs of lovers. Absorbed in his own feelings, Asa merely senses that something is wrong. Potentially complex or interesting events are perceived through a keyhole by an old servant or excitedly reported by others or by messenger. Third, he is an inadequate interpreter of the action. Asa's response to the others' misfortunes, as it is to his own "mean life," is a hapless resignation, a generalized lament on the evils of the times, and a repeated disapproval of the younger generation. Standing somewhat apart from the plot, Asa is made the irritable mouthpiece of an aging, invalid author who found much to dislike in the world.

Because it was in 1942 a Pulitzer Prize–winning novel, one that was also made into a film, *In This Our Life* has attracted special notice.[10] Some critics have sought to overlook its faults and to treat it as a distinguished work. It is in fact inferior to some of Glasgow's earlier books that the public appreciated less. Even more than *Vein of Iron* it betrays the author's fatigue. At its worst it is diffuse and overblown— especially in its aggrieved expressions of self-pity, malaise, and invective against the world and the young. The quality of the writing often seems hasty, verging on slickness. The sections about love, especially, resemble the more hackneyed examples of popular fiction. Glasgow's besetting problem, that of making her characters more than ideas or representatives of social or moral positions, here is particu-

larly evident. Except for the desperate and defiant
Roy, the others are cardboard figures: the selfish sex
kitten, the tycoon, the domineering invalid, the tired
and embittered old man. Locked into her pessimistic
view of society, Glasgow portrays the declining social
order as a contest between evasive idealists and new
people—both flawed, both directionless. Although
she claims that the imminent war made things worse,
this point is not explored.

In This Our Life merits some scrutiny of the
issues it raised, however. Its flavor is more modern
than those earlier works that Glasgow thought of as
realistic social documents. Here she tackles the family, marriage, sex, women's position, the plight of the
Negro, the American obsession with material gain,
and the control of culture by technology. She is bitter
about what she termed "the conspiracy of family
life" and seeks to expose the family as the seat of
personal, psychological, and social ills. She ponders
the decay of confidence in traditional marriage and
the willingness to experiment, however disastrously,
with forms of "open marriage." She pinpoints the
deliberate use of sex as a vindictive expression on the
part of women in revolt against "traditions, or institutions, or conventions . . . or love." She observes the
helplessness of women functioning in a man's world,
where males esteem female sexuality, turpitude, and
weakness over intelligence and independence. She
judges Americans to be preoccupied with a culture
dictated by science and technology, which the novel
translates into the worship of the automobile, the
infatuation with speed and the inescapable caco-
phony of urban daily life. She sounds a new note, for
her, about Southern blacks, deploring the debased
forms of justice and opportunity meted out to them.
An interesting rather than a good novel, *In This Our
Life* leaves us, as Glasgow's last fiction published in

her lifetime, with her sense of the dislocation of contemporary life, through issues that continue to concern American writers, even though her treatment
of them now seems severely limited.

Beyond Defeat (1966)

In July, 1942, three years before her death, Glasgow
wrote that she was "trying my hand [at] a short sequel to *In This Our Life*. So many readers missed the
point of that book that I should like to do a less subtle
approach. . . . But I am not sure that this sequel will
ever be published."[11] She insisted that her main characters were not pessimistic. Roy's wild sexual act has
"served as a flare of light in the darkness of her own
mind";[12] Asa is "not a failure in life, but a man in
whom character, not success, was an end in itself."[13]
Beyond Defeat, a novel that covers a single day, she
hoped would clarify this.

It is autumn, 1942. Roy returns after three
years to Queenborough. She is twenty-six. With her
is her child, Timothy, the offspring of her single
reckless night with a stranger. Illness, loneliness,
and hard work have dogged her. She has had pneu-
monia while working in a New York basement and
now needs to find someone to care for Timmy while
she goes to the Adirondacks to be healed. Despite
all, Roy is inspired to courage by her beautiful son
and feels that life yet has much for her. "She had
fought on beyond defeat, and she had won the kind
of peace that is victory."

Stanley is in California. Uncle Fitzroy has died,
leaving money to Lavinia, Roy's invalid mother. Her
father now lives with Kate Oliver at Hunter's Fare.
Suntanned and healthy with his out-of-doors work,
Asa enjoys his freedom. Craig, too, lives on Kate's

farm community, though he is soon to leave for the
Navy. When relatives refuse, Kate comes through
and agrees to take the little boy, "Asa's grandchild,"
until Roy's second return.

Roy renews her bond with Craig. The three together, Craig, Roy, and Timmy, seem to form a family. They are soon to be divided but look to a reunion
in an undefined future. Lavinia dies at the last, and
the remaining family together reflect on the passing
of an era, a tradition from which they can salvage
"the living seeds of tomorrow."

The novel's beginning is not only a homecom-
ing, a return to a place of rootedness, but astonish-
ingly like a return from the grave. The main character, having passed through death's sickly shadow,
seems to rise again to a new paradisal world. "She
had lived and died and been born over again." She
has experienced a "resurrection of the body." Asa,
too, like one who has "fought . . . through the dark
forest," looks "as if he had been to the end of his life,
and had come out somewhere else, in another beginning."

The beauty of the natural scene is emphasized.
Strong Kate is an earth mother, who seems to be "a
part of the autumn," "her nature . . . rooted in some
hidden identity with the land." There is the reconciliation with an idealized father as the returning
daughter exclaims, "my deepest roots are in you,
Daddy." The whole is a mythic reunion with what to
Glasgow was the perfected family—the benevolent,
tender father, the healthy mother, the undemanding
and not yet carnal spouse, and the beautiful child
whose physical origins are vague. Indeed it is a family
that Glasgow never had.

However, this reunion is only a fleeting glimpse
of eternity, not eternity itself. The group is to dis-

solve and disperse. Asa perceives the flow, "the changeless, perpetual, rhythm of time passing:

Clouds and light, air and water, tree and flower, all were drifting. . . . For it was the closing season of an abundant earth, when nature, serene and effortless, was drifting into the long pause of winter . . . .

The child betokens "mystery" and "the unknown." He belongs "not with the buried past but with that endless becoming which was the unknown, and as yet unborn, future." Glasgow, sketching out the brief novel that would be her last, ill and writing only in gasps, nonetheless could say of the gathering, "This is peace, she thought; I have suffered enough. This is the end of strain and violence, and of wanting that is not ever satisfied."

This novel is of biographical rather than literary interest, for its lineaments are those of dream and desire. Throughout her last losing struggle with ill health, Glasgow withdrew ever more from reality, finding consolation in the ancient idea of eternal returns. She imposes the cyclic pattern of death and rebirth on *Beyond Defeat.* Her characters brush with mortality; they emerge renewed in a place of natural beauty where the earth holds forth freshness, and for the author a promise of rest.

9

○○○○○○○○○○○○○○○○○○○○○○○○○○○○○○○○○○

Poems and Short Stories

The Poems

Fifty-six poems that Glasgow had written during her twenties were collected and published as *The Free-man and Other Poems* (1902) after the appearance of her fourth novel. She had composed "England's Greatness" at the tomb of her admired Charles Darwin. Other verses are filled with images of struggle, battle, rebellion, madness, pessimism, and death, reflections of her "morbid sensitiveness." The title poem, written when she was twenty-two, indicates that the slave who hopes for freedom is yet a slave, while only "Despair is a freeman." The poet sees herself variously as a fighter, a lunatic, a lonely traveller through a dark storm, and a hunter plundering the graves of the dead in her quest for truth:

> In graves of mouldered love and lust,
> I search for secrets of the dust

"Love Has Passed Along The Way" signals the loss of love as a "corpse upon the bed." The religious poems show her defying the God of tradition. "To a Strange God" denounces that deity's wrath and vengeance. In "The Vision of Hell," the poet declares that if God chooses only certain of the strong to be saved, she will take her stand beside the weak and the sinful:

"The damned I choose." However, as Glasgow
moved toward mysticism in her reading, she acknowledged in "A Creed" her belief in "all souls
luminous with love, / Alike in Buddha and in Christ."
Her sense of the "fellowship of living things" includes all creatures and plants. Several poems, such
as "Justice" and "To My Dog", express her feeling for
animals. In a fervent and compassionate vein is her
hymn to the Virgin Mary.

Glasgow considered her verses strong and un-
conventional. Reviewers found them extreme. One
condemned their tendency toward "cheap tragical
utterance,"[1] and the book sold poorly. She produced
no other volumes of poems but did not abandon poetry altogether. Three poems appeared in *Harper's
Magazine* for April, 1908, and June, 1912. Her verses
on woman's suffrage, "The Call" appeared in *Colliers
Magazine* in 1912. The poems must be judged of
slight literary interest today. For the student of Glasgow, they shed light on her personal anguish as a
young woman, her sense of herself as a rebel, and her
attempts to resolve her religious doubts.

The Short Stories

Early in Glasgow's career, her editor, Walter Hines
Page, urged her to put her best efforts in her novels,
and for the most part she followed his advice:

I shall write no more short stories and I shall not divide my
power or risk my future reputation. I will become a great
novelist or none at all. For which determination you are in
part responsible.[2]

It is true that she liked to explore history, heredity, the long, unfolding causes of things. For this she
needed the spaciousness of the novel; the compres-

sion the short story demanded was less congenial. After publishing three stories in her early career, she did not publish another for seventeen years. The remaining ten were written or appeared between 1916 and 1924, a period during which her novel writing was at a low ebb. The stories' main interest lies in their treatment of themes that she developed more fully and skillfully in the novels.

The stories are of three general types, with some overlapping. There is the ethical dilemma story "A Point in Morals." Eight stories are about the difficult and rarely happy relations between men and women, and four are tales of the uncanny and the supernatural, with a psychic emphasis. These four led reviewers to compare Glasgow to Henry James and Edgar Allan Poe. With Poe, a Richmond writer, Glasgow confessed she felt an affinity.

Possibly the need for money as well as the feeling of creative slump impelled Glasgow to turn to stories once again after renouncing the genre. At any rate, she sold nearly all to women's magazines such as *Good Housekeeping* or to journals of more general literary interest like *Harper's* and *Scribner's*.

STORIES WRITTEN BEFORE 1900

Glasgow's first published story, "A Woman of Tomorrow" (*Short Stories: A Magazine of Fact and Fiction*, August, 1895) explores the conflict between work and art that surfaces in three of her novels. The heroine is a young attorney, a Yale honors graduate. She renounces her Virginia lover's pleading to "become a woman for his sake, suffer as other women suffer . . . merge her identity to his." A decade later when she is about to be appointed a Supreme Court justice, she feels suddenly tired. The sight of a nursing mother in the street stirs her emotionally. She returns home to find her old love married, his wife "a small, tired woman in a soiled gown, with a child upon her shrunken breast." The relieved heroine thanks God for her decision and turns her back once and for all on romance.

In "Between Two Shores" (*McClure's Magazine*, February, 1899), a young Southern widow, Lucy Smith, meets on shipboard a cynical yet attentive stranger who claims that his name is L. Smith. The other passengers suppose them to be married. They fall in love. At the end of the crossing he confesses that he is hunted for a murder, though it was "a deed of honor." In anguish Lucy sobs alone, "It was so short." Before they disembark to part forever, she allows the deception that he is her husband to continue so that he can temporarily evade pursuers in Liverpool. This story, written after her first trip to Europe in 1896, shows Glasgow toying with the characterization of the sexually vital man who both attracts and menaces. Such alluring males appeared in all three of her novels about the woman artist.

"A Point in Morals" (*Harper's Magazine,* May, 1899) is also a shipboard narrative involving a criminal. A group of ocean passengers converse about topics ranging from civilization to the value of human life. The situation resembles those intellectual discussions at the Gotham Hotel in *Phases of an Inferior Planet.* A doctor then tells his story. He once shared a train ride with a wanted killer who recounted his own harried life story—the women he had loved, the treacherous colleague he had shot. The man, intent upon suicide, possessed only a vial of acid; this would ensure a horrible death. He pleaded with the doctor to leave him a packet of morphine instead so he could die painlessly. The doctor made what he considered a "sincere" and "conscientious" decision: He placed the drug on the seat before getting off the train. The suicide was in the next day's paper. The shipboard hearers of the tale exclaim and comment upon the story, although no real resolution of the moral question is reached. We do not learn the author's opinion. But in later stories she was to create "sincere" physican characters whose egotism or insensitivity are depicted unsympathetically.

LATER STORIES: 1916—1924

Stories about Men and Women

"Thinking Makes It So" (*Good Housekeeping,* February, 1917) tells of a faded, self-effacing librarian of forty-three. Margaret French is also a writer who supports herself, her nieces, and her widowed invalid sister. The sister, who spends her life on the sofa, is a version of the ladylike hypochondriac seen in so many of the novels. When Margaret receives the first of several fan letters from a plain man with a poetic sensibility, her life is transformed. A railroad builder in Colorado, he has read her poetry and loves her from afar. Glasgow here spiritualizes the rugged Western hero of *Life and Gabriella.* Margaret changes her hair, wears a rose-colored dress, and radiates an inner light while the family, grown accustomed to her martyred role, becomes awed and suspicious. When the man insists on coming to meet her, she tremblingly faces him in her own drawing room. So changed is she by his homage that he happily finds her "beautiful . . . just as I dreamed of you."

Aspects of her own experience undoubtedly gave Glasgow the idea for this sugary story. She was herself forty-three. She had recently fallen in love with Henry Anderson. She may have wondered whether the greatest part of her emotional energy

was being given to her art. As in some of the earlier
novels, she again plays—though more romantically—
with the possibility that within a single woman the
artist and the beloved might be happily fused.

"The Difference" (*Harper's Magazine*, June,
1923), constructs a favorite triangle, that in which
two women compete for a faithless man. Margaret
Fleming's husband of twenty years has a young mistress, Rose Morrison. Rose writes to the wife, asking
to see her. She proposes that Margaret give up
George, the husband, for his sake.

In the interim, a guarded conversation takes
place between Margaret and a woman friend in
which Glasgow airs some of her views: that "women
love with their imagination and men with their
senses"; that men are incapable of constancy; and
that in the world's malicious eyes a man at forty-five
still has plenty of life and adventure ahead of him,
while a woman of the same age is through.

Margaret visits Rose, whom she sees as hard,
young, and slovenly, her mouth painted "like raw
flesh." Rose sees Margaret as Victorian and incapable
of understanding George. An artist, Rose believes
love is necessary to her "self-development." When
Margaret, shocked and sobered, offers George his
freedom, she finds he doesn't want it. The affair with
Rose is to him only "sort of—recreation." Margaret
feels sympathy for Rose, with whom she sees herself
"united . . . by the bond of woman's immemorial
disillusionment." Written while she was working on
Barren Ground, the story reflects Glasgow's own disappointment. It also anticipates the conspiracy between those mutual users, the adulterous husband
and the sexually liberated girl, that would form an
essential element of *The Sheltered Life*. Like many
of her fictions, it reveals the man as inferior to the
women he betrays.

The Victorian and the modern woman clash
again in "The Artless Age" (*The Saturday Evening
Post*, August, 1923), but here they are both young.
Mary Louise is "a nice girl" with "a Victorian aura"
who grows roses and plays croquet. Flippant Geraldine is rouged and slangy; she brags about how she
sips her dates' whiskey out of a flask at dances. Both
girls vie for the well-bred young Richard. But Mary
Louise, who feigns an ankle injury so that she can
languish charmingly on a sofa, shows herself to be
designing. Straightforward Geraldine, however out-
rageous, wins Richard. Geraldine's correct and elderly widowed father finds Mary Louise exactly to his
taste and chooses her. This amusing if obvious tale
bears a competent relation to the style of the novels
of manners. The same distinction between the prim
girl and the flapper is made in *One Man in His Time*.

"Jordan's End," which first appeared in Glasgow's collection *The Shadowy Third and Other Stories* (1923), is one of her three old plantation tales in
a Southern Gothic mode. Jordan's End is a crumbling
manse set in a tangle of ivy, moss, and boxwood. In
it dwell several bizarre members of the Jordan family, particularly a thin, decaying beauty, Miss Judith,
and her mad husband. A doctor is summoned to care
for the husband. When he returns, he finds that
Judith has allowed her husband to take a fatal overdose of a medically prescribed opiate. But the difficulty of proving whether a crime has indeed been
committed prevents her being prosecuted.

The motif of the lethal overdose had appeared in
the early tale, "A Point in Morals," and the moral
dilemma of that tale is faintly echoed here. But two
important themes surface that are more pertinent to
Glasgow's overarching interest, both concerning the
strong woman character. The Southern lady's ability
quietly to commit crimes with impunity appears in

The Ancient Law, The Sheltered Life, and *In This Our Life.* Even more dear to the author's heart is the woman of superior strength who, one way or the other, manages to survive while watching her lover or husband die wretchedly.

"Romance and Sally Byrd" appeared in *The Woman's Home Companion* for December, 1924, and was reprinted in *World's Best Short Stories,* 1925. Sally Byrd has a humdrum life. She agrees to "go away in secret" with a man she loves, only to find that he is already married, although separated. Crushed, she parts from him and will wait for his divorce. Upon learning that he has been in an accident, Sally Byrd lies her way into his luxurious apartment house, pretending to be the nurse. She confronts her lover's middle-aged, graying wife, who is darning his socks and looking like all those other Glasgow women who have "finished with love."

The wife murmurs some cynical truisms: "Marriage for some men, you know, is merely a prop to lean against when they need a support." Sally Byrd goes back to Virginia. She decides that she is through with romance but recovers a little when she meets an attractive man on the train. Another triangular tale like "The Difference," this sprightly specimen of popular fiction shows Glasgow's ability to treat the same topic with humor as well as pathos.

"The Professional Instinct" remained unpublished until 1963.[3] Dr. Estbridge detests his overfed and overbearing wife, who interferes in every aspect of his life, including his profession. He feels himself in revolt "against the whole world of women," feeling they are "victorious over the lives and destinies of men." When he is passed over—through his wife's machinations—for an important promotion, he decides to take a post in the Far East and begin life anew. He romantically asks Judith Campbell, the gentle, yielding woman he loves, to accompany him.

Although she has just been offered the presidency of a midwestern college, she throws it over in a moment to go with Estbridge. Despite his elation, the thwarting of his professional hopes still rankles. When, on the same day, the coveted promotion becomes available at the local hospital, the incumbent having died suddenly, ambition gets the better of Estbridge. The story ends with his deep hesitation, even though taking the job would mean betraying the woman who gave up her profession for his sake.

Another sardonic tale of two women and a man, this one also takes up the conflict between work and love that had interested Glasgow in her earliest novels. Here both the man and the woman face the same dilemma; the woman can be counted on to choose love, whereas it appears that the man will choose work. There are obvious flaws. Chiefly, Glasgow has difficulty in making a plausible character of the lovable professional woman, for she had stereotypical ideas of femininity that she considered indispensable. A philosophy professor aiming for a college presidency, Judith is too pliable and Victorian, too full of "delicate graces" to be credible. Nor is it convincing that she would impulsively give up all for the peevish, selfish Estbridge. Glasgow exchanged letters about the story with Dr. Pearce Bailey, a physician friend in New York. If it had any personal allusion to their relationship, this might have been an added reason to avoid publication. The tale's feminist interest lies in its suggestion that Glasgow strove to exorcize the dominant woman by making her a monster and to create an idealized feminine intellectual type.

Stories of the Supernatural

Three of the four supernatural stories also touch on relationships between men and women, a subject

central to Glasgow's work as a whole. All are recounted in the first person by a reliable narrator, a
technique intended to enhance credibility. The
ghosts have a purpose beyond simply inspiring horror. Either they reveal a connection between the
past and the present, or they convey some psychological truth about the living characters—those who see
the ghost and those who do not.

The first of these tales was "The Shadowy Third"
(*Scribner's Magazine,* December, 1916); it was the
title story in Glasgow's collection of 1923. The narrator, Miss Randolph, is engaged as a private nurse to
the nervous wife of a famous surgeon, Dr. Roland
Maradick. The surgeon is rich, magnetic, idolized by
women. Rumor has it that the marriage is loveless
and that the surgeon is only waiting for his wife to die
so that he can inherit her fortune and marry another
woman. Mrs. Maradick has hallucinations, it seems,
of her dead child playing with its toys about the
house. She tells the nurse that the doctor had caused
the child's death so as to increase his own inheritance. Miss Randolph has, however, already seen the
child's ghost, which appears as an elfin little girl in
Victorian plaids. The ghost must be believed in. Miss
Randolph pleads with Dr. Maradick and a medical
colleague of his not to take away the wife, who she
believes is sane. But the men of medicine, awesome
in their power over their patient, hasten her to an
asylum, where she dies.

Miss Randolph stays on as a secretary. One mid-
night, having dined with his fiancée, Dr. Maradick
comes home and ascends the stairs. Summoned
down again almost immediately by the telephone, he
trips, pitches headlong downstairs, and is instantly
killed at the bottom of the flight. In the half-light, the
nurse has perceived a child's jump rope coiled in the
bend of the stair.

This well-made story is one of Glasgow's best. Her narrator is both sensible and impressionable. She sees the ghost before knowing the child has died. Yet she is also capable of becoming emotionally involved with all the Maradicks: She cherishes the ghost; she sympathizes with Mrs. Maradick; she is both attracted to the surgeon and angry with him. Her resentment is twofold: first for his cruelty to his wife, and secondly for ignoring her, Miss Randolph. There is some hint that she even feels a share of guilt for his death. She saw the rope an instant before he tripped; she wanted to reach the light switch, to warn him, she says, although the sudden flooding of the light might have startled him into losing his balance. The mingling of the ghost's will with the narrator's own gives this tale a rich psychic dimension.

Encouraged by her success and assured that there was a market for the supernatural, Glasgow went on to write "Dare's Gift" (*Harper's Magazine*, February and March, 1917). The title refers to an isolated plantation, its history extending to colonial times. The Virginia owners do not wish to live in it. The narrator is Beckwith, a lawyer who leases the house for himself and his unstable wife. The house feels strange to both. The wife unaccountably betrays her husband by leaking a scandalous business secret of his to the papers. Beckwith is now convinced of her insanity. But an old neighborhood doctor says that the house is responsible. Other sensitive persons have succumbed "to the psychic force of its memories." He recounts tales of treachery associated with the place. The chief story is that of a Southern belle who had allowed her Northern lover to be captured and shot, thinking he had secrets that might save the Confederacy.

The woman who destroys her lover is a familiar type in Glasgow's fiction. Here, however, the motive is impersonal. The obsession with the Confederate cause, even when all but lost, is seen as a force that might not only unhinge minds (as with Mrs. Blake in *The Deliverance*), but that could and did linger on in the present day. The atmosphere of Dare's Gift, however preternatural, is capable of an almost symbolic interpretation of the way in which the past permeates the present.

"The Past" appeared in *Good Housekeeping* for October, 1920, and was included in *Best Short Stories of 1921*. Events are recounted by Miss Wrenn, secretary to the wealthy Mrs. Vanderbridge. Miss Wrenn feels the mystery of the house, a luxurious dwelling off Fifth Avenue in New York. Both she and her employer are able to see the mist-clad ghost of the first Mrs. Vanderbridge, who joins them at the dining table whenever the husband's thoughts dreamily wander to her. The ghost glides through the rooms as well; its aspect is malignant. Mrs. Vanderbridge's health declines. One day, directed by her employer to clean out a desk that had belonged to the first wife, Miss Wrenn comes upon a cache of love letters, which she turns over to Mrs. Vanderbridge. They discover that the first wife had received them from a lover after her marriage. Should not the letters be shown to the husband, so that the phantom can be exorcized? Then he might see his first wife as she really was. Instead, Mrs. Vanderbridge burns the letters. The phantom reappears in the room, its mien cleared, beneficent. The explanation is offered: "She had changed the thought of the past, in that lay her victory."

Like "Dare's Gift," the story creates a sense of the past so sinister that it infects the present. Both stories suffer from the officious intrusions of the author, who eagerly wishes to rationalize the mystery and turn the ghost fiction into a story of ideas.

"Whispering Leaves" (*Harper's Magazine,* January and February, 1923) is another plantation ghost story. Again there is a reliable narrator, Miss Effie. She comes to visit her distant cousins in the Virginia country house where her mother and several grandmothers were born. She herself has never been in Virginia. The family, it is said, has "run to seed." There are unusual things about the place. The groves are unnaturally full of twittering birds. The black servants won't stay after sundown, nor will they work in the fields close to the house.

Miss Effie observes the pale orphaned boy, Pell, being lovingly tended by a noble-featured black woman in a turban. This is the ghost of his old Mammy Rhody (the name inspired by Glasgow's mother's nurse Rhoda). It is she who tamed the birds. The woman haunts the narrator, as if Rhody had belonged to some "half-forgotten childhood which haunted me like a dream." Had she been her mother's mammy as well? When a fire breaks out in the house, Effie beholds the ghost carrying Pell from the flames. She reaches out her arms and takes the child as the ghost melts away. Effie becomes Pell's guardian, thus fulfilling Pell's directive that she is to take him from Whispering Leaves. As in other of the ghost stories, the supernatural is explained as the legacy of memory.

Glasgow wrote of actual ghosts chiefly in her short stories. An exception is the "haunts' walk" around Jordan's Journey in *The Miller of Old Church.* But "shut in, alone, with the past," Glasgow was at home with the ghosts of sad family memories at 1 West Main. She sometimes thought of them as her only companions. As a child, Glasgow found cemeteries her "favorite haunts"; they were romantic to her then and as an adult. But the real ghost that shadows her writing is the Southern past.

○○○○○○○○○○○○○○○○○○○○○○○○○○○○○○

Afterword: The Achievement of Ellen Glasgow

Ellen Glasgow has a permanent significance in American literature as the first writer of the modern South, to which she helped give literary definition in its epoch of social and industrial change. The Virginia of her fiction becomes a paradigm for the region and its history. Summing up the pre-Civil War aristocratic plantation life with its graces and privileges, she wrote a farewell indictment of that life that is nevertheless permeated with regret for the loss of its cultural traditions. The most carefully perceived and wrought of her characters are her women, acting as they do under the stress of their social and biological condition. Stylistically and structurally a writer whose models were Victorian, Glasgow creates a subject matter that prepares the way for her successors, the major Southern writers of our century.

Six of her novels have enduring value. The two finest works of her early period, *The Deliverance* and *The Miller of Old Church,* are romances of the post-Reconstruction South, the one brooding, the other bright and exuberant. *Virginia* stands as a major naturalist novel, in which feminine domestic history is revealed in its crushing subjection to social and sexual forces. *Barren Ground,* while flawed by a failure of ironic distance, remains a work that richly evokes the region, and is still cherished by some readers.

With *The Romantic Comedians,* a sparkling satire on a classic theme, and *The Sheltered Life,* whose satire is darkly pessimistic, Glasgow gave us her last great novels.

Notes

INTRODUCTION

1. "The Dynamic Past," *The Reviewer*, (March 15, 1921), 73–80; *The Letters of Ellen Glasgow*, ed. Blair Rouse (New York: Harcourt, Brace, 1958), letter to Van Wyck Brooks, October 4, 1939, p. 257; *The Woman Within* (New York: Harcourt, Brace, 1954), p. 195; *A Certain Measure: An Interpretation of Prose Fiction* (New York: Harcourt Brace, 1943), p. 30.
2. *A Certain Measure*, p. 155.
3. *Let Me Lie: Being in the Main an Ethnological Account of the Remarkable Commonwealth of Virginia and the Making of Its History* (New York: Farrar, Straus and Co., 1947), p. 261; Geismar, "Ellen Glasgow: The Armor of the Legend," in *Rebels and Ancestors: The American Novel 1890–1915* (Boston: Houghton Mifflin 1953), p. 234.
4. *The Letters of Ellen Glasgow*, Letter to Daniel Longwell [Spring 1932], p. 116.
5. Letter of Allen Tate to Donald Davidson, December 12, 1929, cited in Michael O'Brien, *The Idea of the American South, 1920–1941* (Baltimore: The Johns Hopkins Press, 1979), p. 146.
6. Allen W. Becker, "Ellen Glasgow's Social History," *Texas Studies in English*, 36 (1957), 12–19.
7. Two Virginia writers stand out. John Pendleton Kennedy had in *Swallow Barn* (1832) written appreciatively of the antebellum plantation. Later, Thomas Nelson Page captured the humorous dialect of the freed blacks reminiscing about the good old

days of "Mars Chan" and "Meh Lady" (1884). There was also a wealth of elegiac writing that harked back to a golden epoch of "befo' the wah" or commemorated the glorious defeat.

8. *Life on the Mississippi* (1883), Chap. 46.

9. *A Certain Measure,* p. 138.

10. Kazin, *On Native Grounds* (New York: Harcourt, Brace, 1942), p. 258; Cabell, *Of Ellen Glasgow: An Inscribed Portrait* (New York: The Maverick Press, 1938).

11. C. Vann Woodward, *The Origins of the New South, 1877–1913* (Baton Rouge: University of Louisiana Press, 1951), p. 436.

12. *No Place On Earth: Ellen Glasgow, James Branch Cabell, and Richmond-In-Virginia* (Austin: University of Texas Press, 1959), p. 44.

13. *A Certain Measure,* p. 69.

14. *Let Me Lie,* pp. 236–237.

15. Monique Parent Frazee, "Ellen Glasgow as Feminist," in *Ellen Glasgow: Centennial Essays,* ed. M. Thomas Inge (Charlottesville: University Press of Virginia, 1976), pp. 167–189; Dorothy Scura, "The Southern Lady in the Early Novels of Ellen Glasgow," *Mississippi Quarterly,* 31 (1977–1978), 17–31; Barbro Ekman, *The End of A Legend: Ellen Glasgow's History of Southern Women* (Uppsala, Sweden: Almqvist & Wiksell International, 1979); Anne Goodwyn Jones, *Tomorrow is Another Day: The Woman Writer in the South, 1859–1936* (Baton Rouge: Louisiana State University Press, 1981). Cabell's remarks are in *The New York Herald-Tribune Books,* April 20, 1930.

16. *The Letters of Ellen Glasgow,* letter of July 24, 1941 to Marjorie Kinnan Rawlings, pp. 286–287.

1. "THE MANY TRAGEDIES OF MY LIFE"

1. *The Woman Within* (New York: Harcourt Brace & World, 1954), p. 139. Reissued in paperback (New York: Hill and Wang, 1980).

2. *The Letters of Ellen Glasgow*, ed. Blair Rouse (New York: Harcourt Brace & World, 1958), p. 329, letter of August 14, 1945 to Signe Toksvig. See also *The Woman Within*, p. 16, where Glasgow explains: "Even in childhood, my soul was a battleground for hostile forces."

   The Tidewater aristocracy was identified with Virginia's coastal plain, colonized from the seventeenth century by British gentlemen rather than radicals and zealots. They formed a politically orthodox self-styled aristocracy, supported the English crown against Parliament, and belonged to the Episcopal Church. Virginia's nickname of Old Dominion came from the commonwealth's continued recognition of Charles II after the execution of Charles I. Glasgow described her region as the most English part of the American scene. (Letter to Hugh Walpole, January 9, 1920, Berg Collection, New York Public Library.)

3. Obituary notice clipping, undated. Ellen Glasgow Papers, #5060, Manuscripts Department, University of Virginia Library.

4. *Letters*, Letter to Bessie Zaban Jones (July 20, 1942), pp. 303–304.

5. *The Woman Within*, pp. 85, 87.

6. John Calvin (d. 1564) was a Protestant religious leader whose teachings stressed human sinfulness, distrust of pleasure, close adherence to Scripture, an exacting moral code, and salvation available only to those elected by God, termed the "élite." Although Glasgow resisted her father's ideas and rejected in her personal life what she considered a religion based on fear, her father's qualities nonetheless influenced her thinking. She usually ascribes the Calvinist outlook to her overworked female characters of impoverished status. These include both serious and humorous characters. Harsh views on sexual and married happiness or enjoyment of any kind, a profound mistrust of human nature, which the humble often call "natur', " and the stern religious principles of these women become translated, however, into

different terms when bequeathed to their offspring. Instead of their mothers' fundamentalist religious beliefs, these children inherit fortitude, determination, an infinite willingness to do hard work, and, most importantly, the capacity to survive. Among the children of Calvinist mothers are Dorinda Oakley *(Barren Ground),* Abel Revercomb *(The Miller of Old Church),* Ben Starr *(The Romance of A Plain Man),* and Milly Burden *(They Stooped to Folly).* Ada Fincastle *(Vein of Iron)* inherits her strength from her Calvinist grandmother.

7. The *Woman Within,* p. 193.

8. Ernst Haeckel (1834–1919) was a German naturalist and philosopher, an early proponent of the theory of evolution, who applied its principles to philosophical and religious problems. English translations of his works include *The History of Creation* (1892), quoted by Glasgow at the beginning of *The Descendant,* and *The Struggle over Ideas Concerning Evolution* (1906). August Weismann (1834–1914) was a German biologist and Darwinian evolutionist who argued that acquired characteristics could not be transmitted. A character in Glasgow's novel *The Descendant* is reading his *Essays Upon Heredity and Kindred Biological Problems* (1889, 1892). Edward Gibbon (1737–1794) was an English historian, author of *The Decline and Fall of the Roman Empire* (1776–1788), of which Glasgow's father disapproved. John Stuart Mill (1806–1873) was an English philosopher, political theorist, economist, and author of *On Liberty* (1859), *The Subjection of Women* (1869), and *Utilitarianism* (1863). Walter Bagehot (1826–1877) was an English journalist, political thinker, and economist, editor of *The Economist.* His *Physics and Politics* (1872) sought to apply principles of evolution to the growth of societies. Herbert Spencer (1820–1903) was an English philosopher a popularizer of Darwin, and author of *The Data of Ethics* (1879) and *The Genesis of Science and the Factors of Organic Evolution* (1854). To him we owe the term "survival of the fittest."

Thomas Henry Huxley (1825–1895) was an agnostic English biologist who supported Darwinism against religious orthodoxy. He was an educator and civil servant, author of *Man's Place in Nature* (1863), and *Evolution and Ethics* (1893). Charles R. Darwin (1809–1882) an English naturalist and philosopher, wrote *The Origin of Species* (1859), which Glasgow acknowledged as "the cornerstone of my creed," and *The Descent of Man* (1871). Glasgow's father considered Darwin's ideas "sinister." Glasgow's use of Darwinian thought is analysed in J.R.R. Raper, *Without Shelter: The Early Career of Ellen Glasgow* (Baton Rouge: Louisiana State University Press, 1971).

For more details on Glasgow's reading, see Carrington C. Tutwiler, Jr., *A Catalogue of The Library of Ellen Glasgow* (Charlottesville: Bibiliographical Society of The University of Virginia, 1969), and Julius R. Raper, "Ambivalence Toward Authority: A Look at Ellen Glasgow's Library, 1890–1906," *Mississippi Quarterly* 31 (Winter, 1977–1978), 5–16.

9.   *The Woman Within*, p. 97.
10. Plotinus was a third-century Roman Neoplatonic philosopher whose writings are treasured by the philosopher in Glasgow's *Vein of Iron*. Glasgow found "anodyne" in his *Enneads* (*The Woman Within*, p. 172). Marcus Aurelius was a second-century Roman Stoic philosopher. Glasgow heavily annotated her George Long translation of his *Thoughts of the Emperor Marcus Aurelius Antoninus*. St. Francis of Assisi (1182–1226) was an Italian monk who founded the Franciscan order. Glasgow followed his footsteps in Italy and felt that the saint's memory "flooded my soul with a spiritual radiance." She read *The Life of St. Francis* by Paul Sabatier. *The Bhagavad-Gita; or, The Lord's Song* was the English translation by Annie Besant (1896) of the sacred Hindu text that Glasgow read. It influenced her ideas about renunciation and purity, the quelling of desire and egoism. The Upanishads are philosophical treatises commenting on the Vedas, the most ancient Hindu sacred writings. Buddha was

the title of the Indian philosopher Gautama Siddhartha (fifth century B.C.), founder of Buddhism. Glasgow read the Upanishads and the Buddhist Suttas in "the plain and prosy English of *The Sacred Books of the East.*" Arthur Schopenhauer (1788–1860) was a German philosopher whose *The World As Will and Idea* (trans. 1859 by T. Bailey Saunders) Glasgow especially admired.

11. Interview with M. Whiting, *The Dearborn Independent,* April 9, 1927.

12. Letter to Van Wyck Brooks, September 2, 1939 (*Letters,* p. 255).

13. Glasgow's *New York Times* articles are "No Valid Reason Against Giving Votes to Women" (March 23, 1913) and "Feminism," (November 30, 1913). "The Call" appeared in *Colliers* on July 27, 1912, and was reprinted in *Current Literature* 53 (November, 1912). The last couplet went:

"Woman calls to woman to awaken! / Woman calls to woman to arise. . . . " See also *The Woman Within,* p. 187.

14. Mary Johnston (1870–1936) and Amélie Rives (1863–1945) were popular, sentimental Virginia writers. Rives's husband, Prince Troubetzkoy, painted Glasgow's portrait. Marjorie Kinnan Rawlings (1896–1953) was a Florida writer best known for her Pulitzer Prize–winning novel *The Yearling* (1938). Howard Mumford Jones (1892–1980) was an American scholar, professor, and critic of literature and culture. Carl Van Vechten (1880–1964) was an American writer, novelist, and literary critic whose work heightened interest in black culture and who also wrote novels of manners set in New York. Allen Tate (1899–1979), a Tennessee writer, poet, and literary critic, helped to found *The Fugitive* (1922–1925) a little magazine of the Southern agrarian cultural movement. Stark Young (1881–1963) was a professor and novelist of the Civil War, a poet, playwright, and drama critic. Van Wyck Brooks (1886–1963) was an American literary critic, editor, teacher, and histo-

rian, whose writing stressed the influence of the Puritan tradition in American culture. Carl Van Doren (1885–1950), Columbia professor, critic, historian, and literary editor of *The Nation*, wrote books on Cabell and Benjamin Franklin, among other subjects. James Branch Cabell (1879–1958) essayist and novelist, was best known for his novel *Jurgen* (1919).

15. Cabell, *As I Remember It: Some Epilogues in Recollection* (New York: McBride, 1955), p. 217. Chap. 30, "Speaks with Candor of a Great Lady," is about Glasgow.

16. Review in *The Nation*, 120 (May 6, 1925), 521. See also *As I Remember It*, pp. 219–223, and *Let Me Lie*, p. 263.

17. Letter to Walter Hines Page, December 2, 1899, *Letters*, pp. 28–29.

18. Edgar E. MacDonald discusses the matter in detail in "The Glasgow-Cabell Entente," *American Literature*, 41 (March 1969), 265–271, and in "An Essay in Bibliography," *Ellen Glasgow: Centennial Essays*, ed. Thomas M. Inge (Charlottesville: University of Virginia Press, 1976), p. 212.

19. *The Letters of James Branch Cabell*, ed. Edward Wagenknecht (Norman: University of Oklahoma Press, 1975), p. 174, letter of August 6, 1941.

20. *The Woman Within*, pp. 153, 178.

21. Rupert Hart-Davis, *Hugh Walpole: A Biography* (New York: Macmillan 1952), p. 281.

22. Reconstruction, a painful time for the South, had been enforced under a Republican administration. After the Civil War, "solid South" meant voting Democratic, though the Democratic Party had meant different things at different periods.

23. Marjorie Kinnan Rawlings, a devoted admirer of Glasgow, had gathered notes for a biography she did not live to write. Her 1953 interview with Anderson and other of Glasgow's Richmond acquaintances is published in E. E. MacDonald's "A Retrospective Henry Anderson and Marjorie Kinnan Rawlings," *Ellen Glasgow Newsletter*, 12 (March 1980), 4–16.

24. Ellen Glasgow Papers, #5060, Manuscripts Department University of Virginia Library.

25. "I Believe," in Clifton Fadiman (ed.), *The Personal Philosophies of Certain Eminent Men and Women of Our Time* (New York: Simon & Schuster, 1938), p. 95.

26. *Let Me Lie*, p. 253.

27. The author's conversation on October 6, 1979, with Josephine Glasgow Clark, Richmond, Va.; "A Retrospective Henry Anderson and Marjorie Kinnan Rawlings," p. 4; Letter of Hugh Walpole to Ellen Glasgow, February 22, 1927, Ellen Glasgow Papers #5060, Manuscripts Department University of Virginia Library; Julian R. Meade, *I Live In Virginia* (New York: Longmans, Green, 1935), p. 183; "A Retrospective Henry Anderson," p. 7; Isaac Marcosson, *Before I Forget: A Pilgrimage to the Past* (New York: Dodd, Mead, 1959), p. 495; Sara Haardt [Mencken], in *Ellen Glasgow: Critical Essays*, ed. Stuart Sherman, Sara Haardt, and Emily Clark (New York: Doubleday, Doran, 1929), p. 15.

28. Louise Maunsell Field, "Miss Glasgow At Home," *The New York Times Book Review and Magazine* (July 30, 1922); Meade, *I Live in Virginia*, p. 183; Alice M. Tyler, "A Woman Author of the South, Ellen Glasgow: Her Books and Her Personality," *The Book News Monthly*, 30 (August, 1912), 1843–1848; Dorothy Scura, "One West Main," *Ellen Glasgow Newsletter*, 1 (October, 1974), 3–6; author's conversation with Josephine Glasgow Clark, October 6, 1979.

29. Cabell, *Let Me Lie*, p. 354; "A Retrospective Henry Anderson," p. 7.

30. Meade, *I Live In Virginia*, p. 185.

31. Maude Williams, Glasgow's friend who had introduced her and Henry Anderson, in an interview with Marjorie Kinnan Rawlings, "A Retrospective Henry Anderson," p. 11.

32. Meade, *I Live In Virginia*, pp. 184–185; Cabell, *As I Remember It*, pp. 219, 231, 234; Meade, *I Live In Virginia*, p. 186; *The Woman Within*, p. 267.

33. *Let Me Lie*, p. 264; *As I Remember It*, pp. 227–229, 233.

34. *The Woman Within,* p. 139; *A Certain Measure* p. 178; *The Woman Within,* p. 213.
35. *Letters of James Branch Cabell,* p. 218, letter of November 3, 1945.

2. THE ARTIST IN NEW YORK

1. In the Gospels, Mary Magdalene was a follower of Jesus. Later, medieval art and legend showed her renouncing a life of prostitution to endure privations in the desert before achieving sainthood. The image of the Magdalene foreshadows Rachel's situation as a woman whom society declares ruined and who is then able to redirect her energies to a higher purpose.
2. Among those of Glasgow's contemporaries most influenced by naturalism were Hamlin Garland, Stephen Crane, Frank Norris, Jack London, and Theodore Dreiser.
3. *The Woman Within,* p. 108.
4. Hamlin Garland, " 'The Descendant' and Its Author," *The Book Buyer,* 15 (August, 1897), p. 45–46. Garland also wrote after meeting her that he expected Glasgow to be "a marked personality in Southern literature" (*Roadside Meetings,* New York: Macmillan, 1930), p. 350.
5. Both are characters in Wagner's operas. Elsa, in *Löhengrin,* marries Löhengrin, a knight of mysterious and exalted origins. In *Tristan und Isolde,* Isolde is the heroine who sacrifices everything—marriage, loyalty to friends, reputation, eventually her life—for love. Both bear a relation to Mariana, whose husband Algarcife (possibly based on an Arabic star-name in the constellation Orion), is described as a special sort of being of the future, almost too splendid for this inferior planet.
6. *The Voice of the People* (1900), *The Battle-Ground* (1902), *The Deliverance* (1904).
7. *The Woman Within,* p. 171.
8. *Rebels and Ancestors,* pp. 238, 236.

3. THE CIVIL WAR AND ITS AFTERMATH

1. *The Letters of Ellen Glasgow*, ed. Blair Rouse (New York, 1958), p. 29, letter of December 2, 1899, to Walter Hines Page. Glasgow's first Virginia novel was *The Voice of The People* (1900). A novel of politics, it is discussed in Chapter 4.
2. Among modern novels are Stark Young's *So Red the Rose* (1934); Margaret Michell's *Gone with the Wind* (1936); William Faulkner's *Absalom, Absalom!* (1936); and Allen Tate's *The Fathers* (1938).
3. *A Certain Measure*, p. 13.
4. These two events occurred a year and a half apart. John Brown, a minister, conducted a raid on the arsenal at Harper's Ferry, October 16–18, 1859. The venture, financed by Northern abolitionists, was an ill-fated effort to emancipate nearly four million slaves. Brevet Colonel Robert E. Lee captured Brown, who was hanged for treason against the state of Virginia.

   In December, 1860, South Carolina seceded in protest against Lincoln's election as President. The U.S. government sent forces to hold South Carolina's Fort Sumter. General P. G. T. Beauregard's firing on Sumter on April 12, 1861 opened the Civil War. Lincoln's determination to call troops in response to the bombardment led Virginia to secede five days later, on April 17, 1861. The Confederate capital was established at Richmond in May.
5. *A Certain Measure*, p. 30.
6. *A Certain Measure*, p. 35.
7. The Reconstruction Acts were administered in the period after the Civil War, from 1867 to 1877. Virginia became an occupied military district. The federal government imposed political and economic measures upon the former Confederate states before allowing them to be readmitted to the Union.

   As for the economic effects of Reconstruction, which are reflected in *The Deliverance*, the emancipation of four million slaves would have reduced most of the planter class to financial ruin. Those who hoped for loans to rebuild their plantations were disappointed when moneys in the Confederate treasuries were confiscated by the North. Plantations, most of them mortgaged before the war, now underwent foreclosure. Many white farmers, previously poor, could profit from the new availability of land and freed black workers. Although there was no such large-scale land redistribution as Glasgow implies, these farmers were often accused of having enriched themselves by collaborating with carpetbaggers. This derogatory term referred to any northerners who came south for business and political reasons, whether good or bad. Certainly not all poor white farmers were unscrupulous; Glasgow, however, portrays Bill Fletcher as a usurper who has come into his wealth by shady means.

8. *A Certain Measure*, p. 29.
9. *A Certain Measure*, p. 35.
10. *A Certain Measure*, pp. 32–33.
11. The Grail legend appears in medieval literature and notably in Sir Thomas Malory's *Morte D'Arthur*. The search for the Grail is conducted by knights who are pure and meritorious. The Grail was a sacred receptacle that fed the hungry and restored the sick. It is associated with humanity's quest for spiritual good, for peace, and the release from suffering.

4. POLITICAL MEN OF VIRGINIA

1. Even before the Civil War, the South was becoming known as Democratic, although what was meant by "Democratic Party" varied with the times. The essentially conservative Democrats had absorbed older aristocratic elements, such as the Southern Whig Party. Because Lincoln was a Republican humanely opposed to slavery, his election in 1860 helped to consolidate, in opposition, a Democratic and secessionist South. The Republican alignment with abolition, and later, its administration of the Reconstruc-

tion Acts, further drew the Democratic "solid South" together. Most Southern blacks voted Republican. The Democratic Party was eventually considered the only one in which a politically ambitious white Southerner could succeed.

After the Civil War, the Democrats' commitment to the South's industrial development as a means to economic recovery meant their cooperating with Yankee business interests. Some Southern Democrats also became commercial entrepreneurs, not above enriching themselves personally while collaborating with the North. Glasgow's novels often draw attention to the corruptness of the Democratic machine, which tends to anger the lower-class and idealistic members of the society.

2. Southern blacks were effectively disenfranchised between 1897 and 1904 by such practices as gerrymandering, literacy tests, and poll taxes. A crafty device of shifting around separate voting boxes for different offices was designed to baffle unsophisticated voters, poor white as well as black. *The Voice of The People* refers to an evil plan to drown a barge full of blacks on their way to the polls. Glasgow's attitude toward blacks is mixed. While she praises Burr's willingness to accept black votes, she elsewhere in the novel alludes disapprovingly to miscegenation: A mulatto is seen slumping in a train, "the degenerate descendant of two races that mix only to decay." She left the line out of a later edition. The blacks in *The Voice of the People* are pleasant and amusing, their dialect wittily reproduced. But beyond affectionately capturing their charming ways, she fails to find a significant social or political place for them.

3. The Populists saw help for farmers through the expanded powers of government; that is, of the people. Challenging the one-party Democratic machine, theirs was a protest against the increasing power of both capitalist financiers and railroad magnates who exerted control from the northeast over the South.

This control involved the corporate ownership of farm land, as well as the charging of high rates to the farmers by railroads even while the prices of their produce dropped. The southern Populist movement of the 1880s and 1890s had a program that included government regulation of railroads and trusts such as the tobacco trust, government-built warehouses for storing nonperishable farm products, credit and loans to farmers, soil conservation, and help to farmers in diversifying their crops. *The Voice of the People* avoids connecting anything so specific with Nick Burr. A Populist attitude is expressed by Nick's father, Amos Burr, but it is used to point up his shiftlessness: "I want my rights, an' I want the country to give 'em to me." His status as a peanut grower accurately reflects the new postwar diversification of crops by small truck farms.

4. Woodrow Wilson (1856–1924), twenty-eighth President of the United States, was in the White House. His term ran from 1913 to 1921. Wilson, a native-born Virginian who had lived in other states as well, was a Democrat. He had studied law at the University of Virginia. By appointing five Southern-born cabinet members as well as many lesser officials in his administration, he had restored the prestige of the Southerner on the national scene. There were more Southerners in Washington during his administration than at any time since the Civil War. Still, there were Southerners who disputed that Wilson was a "true" Southerner.

    Within weeks after his reelection in 1916, Wilson was renewing his efforts to keep America out of the war. But by April 4, 1917, the war resolution was adopted.

5. The view that the Reconstruction acts were excessively harsh was founded in part on an assumption of white racial superiority. Radical Reconstruction was congressionally mandated in Virginia in 1867, and Virginia was made an occupied military district. While blacks had new political privileges, many

whites were disenfranchised, notably those who had
in any way politically supported the Confederacy.
Violent white reaction aggravated Southern negro-
phobia and led directly to the formation of the Ku
Klux Klan after 1869.

6. See Chapter 1. Anderson, a Progressive, also believed
    that his speech of June, 1916, "An American Citi-
    zen," had "direct influence" on Blackburn's ideas.
    Glasgow inscribed his copy of *The Builders* "To
    Henry W. Anderson, with whose help and inspiration
    this book was written. . . ." ("A Retrospective Henry
    Anderson," *Ellen Glasgow Newsletter* 12 [March
    1980], 8).

5. THE GROWTH OF THE NEW SOUTH

1. In the decade between 1880 and 1890, Southern rail-
    road mileage more than doubled. The trend was to
    consolidate the various lines. The Richmond & West
    Point Terminal Company actually did absorb smaller
    subsidiary lines, forming the South's largest railroad.
    This growth is reflected in Ben Starr's vision for the
    Great South Midland and Atlantic of the novel. It
    should be noted that although southerners directed
    the railroads the investors and financial managers
    were largely from the northeast.

2. The Panic of 1893 was precipitated in part by the
    swift overexpansion of the railroads. When the Phila-
    delphia and Reading Railroad went bankrupt, ruin-
    ing many of its creditors, a depression followed. Sev-
    eral railroad companies went into receivership. The
    south Atlantic seaboard was left without a railway
    system when the Richmond & West Point Terminal
    Company failed. Richmond especially suffered from
    widespread unemployment. Strikes and riots fol-
    lowed. The New York financier J. Pierpont Morgan
    purchased at this time the failed Richmond & West
    Point Terminal Company and from it established the
    great Southern Railway. This is reflected in the novel

when the Cumberland and Tidewater Railroad goes "into the hands of a receiver and is bought up easily by the Great South Midland and Atlantic."

3. The novel appeared in the same year that Glasgow became moderately active in the woman's suffrage movement. See chapter 1.

4. *A Certain Measure,* p. 70.

5. *A Certain Measure,* p. 128.

6. VIRGINIA HEROINES

1. *A Certain Measure,* pp. 79, 82, 96.

2. The teachings of St. Paul on women are found in I Corinthians 7; I Corinthians 14: 34–35; I Timothy 2:11; and Ephesians 5:22.

3. *A Certain Measure,* p. 83.

4. *A Certain Measure,* p. 98.

5. *The Letters of Ellen Glasgow,* ed. Blair Rouse (New York: Harcourt, Brace, 1958), p. 69, letter of August 23, 1923, to Hugh Walpole.

6. *Letters,* p. 74, letter of January 26, 1925, to Douglas Southall Freeman.

7. Interestingly, Glasgow attributes to music Dorinda's waves of sexual turmoil at a point in the author's own life when her deafness was acute enough to have prevented her from the enjoyment of music.

8. See, for instance, letters to William H. F. Lamont, February 9, 1928 (*Letters,* p. 90), to Daniel Longwell, July 12, 1932 (*Letters,* p. 118), and to Signe Toksvig, February 4, 1944 (*Letters,* p. 341); *The Woman Within,* p. 243.

9. "The Last Cry of Romance," *The Nation,* 120 (May 6, 1925), 521. On his later maintaining that it was his review and his recognition of Glasgow as a social historian that had given her the idea of the regional and historical plan of her Virginia novels, and his feeling that she had not given him sufficient credit for this insight, see above, Chapter 1.

10. *A Certain Measure,* p. 160.

11. Cabell and others attributed the naming of Jason to the classical legend of Jason and Medea. When Jason leaves her to marry a richer woman, Medea vengefully stifles her maternal feeling and slays her children by Jason. The modern parallel is seen in Jason's betrayal and Dorinda's surpressing her womanly capacity for love and miscarrying Jason's child.

12. It is worth noting how many novels contain the motif of the woman survivor and the weak, depraved, criminal, sick, or alcoholic male: *The Descendent, Life and Gabriella, Barren Ground, The Sheltered Life* (in which the woman kills the man); in *The Romance of a Plain Man, The Romantic Comedians,* and *Vein of Iron,* the woman nurses the sick man.

13. The same likeness is discerned in Michael Akershem in *The Descendent,* an indication that both are ultimately male victim types. As a young woman betrayed, Dorinda initially shares her father's propensities to weakness, but she spends her life surmounting these.

14. The agricultural figure is deliberate. The same passage continues to apply the "barren ground" metaphor to the religious theme: "She had ploughed desperately in the dry and stubborn acres of theology." The "mental harvest" was not one of faith, however, but conduct.

15. *Rebels and Ancestors: The American Novel 1890–1915* (Boston, 1953), pp. 262–263.

16. Praise of agrarian life was of long standing. The earliest writers, from the seventeenth and eighteenth centuries, saw Virginia as a new Eden where the "husbandman" or farmer could labor amid the vines and groves to recover a golden age. Thomas Jefferson had written: "Those who labor in the earth are the children of God." He saw the husbandman as the ideal type in his *Notes on the State of Virginia* (1784).

    The plantation fictions of both before and after the Civil War connected the benevolent aristocratic patriarch to the land. The Georgia poet Sidney

Lanier (1842–1881), in writing of the New South, had envisioned the land of abundance "as Nature's own agricultural fair; rice grows alongside of wheat, corn alongside of sugar-cane, cotton alongside of clover, apples alongside of peaches . . . ; the little valleys everywhere run with living waters, asking grasses and cattle and quiet grist-mills . . . . There a man may find all he needs to nourish and comfort him." (from "The New South," *Scribner's Monthly,* 20 (October 1880), 840–851). Lanier's poem "Corn" celebrated the "stately corn-ranks," a steadfast army of growth facing the imminent destruction that progress in the form of trade and commerce must bring.

A group of poets in the 1920s, among them John Crowe Ransom and Allen Tate, who called themselves The Fugitives, asserted their intention to preserve southern regional culture and tradition against incursions of industrialism and technology. The manifesto *I'll Take My Stand* (1930) took a similar position. Glasgow eventually wrote to Tate that she too found herself turning away from "the raucous voice of the modern industrial South" (Letter of January 30, 1933, *Letters,* p. 127).

17. *A Certain Measure,* p. 153.

7. CHANGING TIMES AND SEXUAL MORES

1. *A Certain Measure,* p. 213.
2. *A Certain Measure,* pp. 211, 221, 237.
3. Review in *Herald Tribune Books,* April 20, 1930. See also *Let Me Lie* (New York, 1947), pp. 243–244. He also commented that Glasgow's writing on the subject amounts to "The Tragedy of Everywoman, As It Was Lately Enacted In The Commonwealth of Virginia."
4. *The Woman Within,* p. 276. Similar wording is found in *A Certain Measure,* p. 211, and *Letters,* p. 90.

5. *A Certain Measure,* p. 211.
6. The novel's theatricality is evident, and there was some talk of turning it into a play. Letter to Samuel S. Sloan, January 21, 1938, *Letters,* p. 231.
7. The Judge may be modelled in part on the lawyer Henry Anderson, Glasgow's fiancé of long standing, who was said to like younger women. There is also a subtle cluster of allusions to her father, the testy old Francis Glasgow, a philanderer with the black maids and would-be suitor at the age of eighty of his nurse, Miss Bennett. Honeywell lusts after the young black girl who makes his bed and finally eyes his nurse with interest. The choice of the name Cordelia for the dead wife recalls Shakespeare's Lear, to whom Glasgow's brother had compared their father. Lear's predatory daughters deprived him of money, servants, and rank while his disowned daughter Cordelia loved him best. It is worth noticing that Honeywell's faithful dead wife is named Cordelia and that he fails to appreciate her until too late, while bestowing his wealth on the unloving, daughterly Annabel.
8. *A Certain Measure,* p. 215.
9. *A Certain Measure,* pp. 224, 237.
10. They appear in the novel *The Vicar of Wakefield* (1766), Chap. 24. Goldsmith (1728–1774) was an Irish playwright, essayist, novelist, and poet.
11. *A Certain Measure,* p. 245.
12. *A Certain Measure,* p. 224.
13. This motif appears in *The Ancient Law,* where a father covers his daughter's guilt for forgery, and in Glasgow's last novel, *In This Our Life,* where a young woman's hit-and-run killing of a child is allowed, with her family's connivance, to cast blame temporarily on an innocent black youth.

8. VIRGINIA BETWEEN TWO WORLD WARS

1. *A Certain Measure,* p. 178.
2. *A Certain Measure,* p. 173.

3. *A Certain Measure,* p. 169.
4. Glasgow had deliberately renounced irony in her approach: "Sophisticated wit and sparkling irony must be drained away from this bare and steady chronicle of simple lives. . . . Satire would have splintered back from the sober bulk of the Presbyterian mind and conscience" (*A Certain Measure,* pp. 178–179).
5. *A Certain Measure,* p. 246.
6. *A Certain Measure,* p. 249.
7. Letter of December 7, 1943 to Frank Morley, *Letters,* p. 340.
8. Citing these words of Roy's in a letter, Glasgow wrote that "the whole theme was condensed into Roy's cry in the last paragraph. . . . All through her confusion and blind groping she was moving toward that search for 'something good,' and all through the book I was writing with that cry in my mind" (Letter of March 28, 1941 to Van Wyck Brooks, *Letters,* p. 283).
9. *A Certain Measure,* p. 255.
10. The prize was awarded, it was widely believed, to make up for the committee's having passed over the superior novel *The Sheltered Life* (1932). The Warner Brothers film of *In This Our Life* was released in 1942 to coincide with the announcement of the Pulitzer Prize. Olivia de Havilland played Roy, as a gentle, homeloving sister, while Bette Davis played a destructive Stanley, finally killed in a car crash. Howard Koch wrote the screenplay and John Huston was the director.

    The film is discussed by S. K. Bathwick, in Gerald Peary and Roger Shatzkin (eds.), *The Modern American Novel and the Movies* (New York: Ungar, 1978), pp. 143–155. Film reviews have been reprinted in the *Ellen Glasgow Newsletter,* 2 (March 1975), pp. 10–12.

    Glasgow wrote to a friend that "Hollywood . . . had entirely missed the point of my novel. I hated the whole thing." (Letter to Bessie Zaban Jones, June 26, 1942, *Letters,* p. 302.)

11. Letter to Bessie Zaban Jones, July 20, 1942, *Letters,*
    p. 304. The novel was edited and published by Lu-
    ther Y. Gore (Charlottesville: University Press of Vir-
    ginia, 1966).
12. *A Certain Measure,* p. 256.
13. Letter to Bessie Zaban Jones, July 20, 1942, *Letters,*
    p. 304.

9. POEMS AND SHORT STORIES

1. *The Nation,* October 9, 1912.
 2. Letter of November 22, 1897, to Walter Hines Page,
    Letters, p. 25.
 3. Richard K. Meeker, ed., *The Collected Stories of
    Ellen Glasgow* (Baton Rouge: Louisiana State Uni-
    versity Press, 1963), pp. 239–253. The story is edited
    from the manuscript in the University of Virginia
    library.

Bibliography

The largest collection of manuscripts pertaining to Ellen Glasgow is in the Alderman Library of the University of Virginia. Other collections are listed in J. Albert Robbins, *American Literary Manuscripts* (2nd ed., Athens: The University of Georgia Press, 1977), p. 127.

WORKS BY ELLEN GLASGOW

"A Woman of To-morrow." In *Short Stories: A Magazine of Fact and Fiction,* 19 (August, 1895), 415–427.

The Descendant. New York: Harper & Brothers, 1897.

Phases of an Inferior Planet. New York: Harper & Brothers, 1898.

The Voice of the People. New York: Doubleday, Page, 1900.

The Freeman and Other Poems. New York: Doubleday, Page, 1902.

The Battle-Ground. New York: Doubleday, Page, 1902.

The Deliverance. New York: Doubleday, Page, 1904.

The Wheel of Life. New York: Doubleday, Page, 1906.

The Ancient Law. New York: Doubleday, Page, 1908.

The Romance of a Plain Man. New York: Macmillan, 1909.

The Miller of Old Church. Garden City, N.Y.: Doubleday, Page, 1911.

Virginia. Garden City, N. Y.: Doubleday, Page, 1913.

Life and Gabriella. Garden City, N. Y.: Doubleday, Page, 1916.

The Builders. Garden City, N. Y.: Doubleday, Page, 1919.

One Man in His Time. Garden City, N. Y.: Doubleday, Page, 1922.

The Shadowy Third and Other Stories. Garden City, N. Y.: Doubleday, Page, 1923.

Barren Ground. Garden City, N. Y.: Doubleday, Page, 1925.

The Romantic Comedians. Garden City, N. Y.: Doubleday, Page, 1926.

They Stooped to Folly. Garden City, N. Y.: Doubleday, Doran, 1929.

The Old Dominion Edition of the Works of Ellen Glasgow. 8 vols. Garden City, N. Y.: Doubleday, Doran, 1929–1933.

The Sheltered Life. Garden City, N. Y.: Doubleday, Doran, 1932.

Vein of Iron. New York: Harcourt Brace & Co., 1935.

The Virginia Edition of the Works of Ellen Glasgow. 12 vols. New York: Charles Scribner's Sons, 1938.

In This Our Life. New York: Harcourt Brace & Co., 1941.

A Certain Measure: An Interpretation of Prose Fiction. New York: Harcourt Brace & Co., 1943.

The Woman Within. New York: Harcourt Brace & Co., 1954.

Letters of Ellen Glasgow. Ed. Blair Rouse. New York: Harcourt Brace & Co., 1958.

The Collected Stories of Ellen Glasgow. Ed. Richard K. Meeker. Baton Rouge: Louisiana State University Press, 1963.

Beyond Defeat: An Epilogue to an Era. Ed. Luther Y. Gore. Charlottesville: University Press of Virginia, 1966.

UNCOLLECTED POEMS AND ESSAYS

"The Immortal." *Harper's Monthly Magazine,* 116 (April, 1908), 697.

"Song." *Harper's Monthly Magazine,* 125 (June, 1912), 103.

"The Call." *Collier's Magazine,* 47 (July 27, 1912), 21.

"No Valid Reason Against Giving Votes to Women." *The New York Times,* March 23, 1913, sec. 6, p. 11.

"Feminism." *The New York Times Review of Books* (November 30, 1913), 656–657.

"Feminism, A Definition." *Good Housekeeping,* 58 (May, 1914), 683.

"The Dynamic Past." *The Reviewer,* 1 (March, 1921), 73–80.

"Impressions of the Novel." *The New York Herald Tribune Books* (May 20, 1928) 1, 5–6.

"The Novel in the South." *Harper's Monthly Magazine,* 158 (December, 1928), 93–100.

"One Way to Write Novels." *The Saturday Review of Literature,* 11 (December 8, 1934), 335, 344, 350.

"Heroes and Monsters." *The Saturday Review of Literature,* 12 (May 4, 1935), 3–4.

"I Believe." In *The Personal Philosophies of Certain Eminent Men and Women of Our Time.* Ed. Clifton Fadiman. New York: Simon & Schuster, 1938.

" 'Literary Realism or Nominalism' by Ellen Glasgow: An Unpublished Essay," Ed. Luther Y. Gore. *American Literature,* 34 (March 1962), 72–79.

WORKS ABOUT ELLEN GLASGOW

Bibliographies

Kelly, William W. *Ellen Glasgow: A Bibliography.* Charlottesville: University Press of Virginia, 1964.

MacDonald, Edgar E. "An Essay in Bibliography." *Ellen Glasgow Centennial Essays.* Ed. M. Thomas Inge. Charlottesville: University Press of Virginia, 1976.

————. "Ellen Glasgow: An Annotated Checklist, 1973–Present." *The Ellen Glasgow Newsletter* 9 (October 1978), 1–14.

Books and Articles

Auchincloss, Louis. "Ellen Glasgow." *Pioneers and Caretakers: A Study of Nine American Women Novelists.* Minneapolis: University of Minnesota Press, 1965.

Cabell, J. B. "Two Sides of the Shielded: A Note as to Ellen Glasgow." In *Some of Us*. New York: Robert M. McBride, 1930.

———. *Of Ellen Glasgow: An Inscribed Portrait*. New York: The Maverick Press, 1938.

———. "Miss Glasgow of Virginia." In *Let Me Lie: Being in the Main an Ethnological Account of the Remarkable Commonwealth of Virginia and the Making of Its History*. New York: Farrar, Straus, 1947.

———. "Speaks With Candor of a Great Lady." In *As I Remember It: Some Epilogues in Recollection*. New York: McBride, 1955.

Clark, Emily. "Ellen Glasgow." *Innocence Abroad*. New York: Alfred A. Knopf, 1931.

Edel, Leon. "Miss Glasgow's Private World." *The New Republic*, 131 (November 15, 1954), 20–21.

Ekman, Barbro. *The End of a Legend: Ellen Glasgow's History of Southern Women*. Acta Universitatis Upsaliensis: Studia Anglistica Upsaliensia, No. 37. Uppsala, Sweden: Almqvist & Wiksell International, 1979.

Geismar, Maxwell. "Ellen Glasgow: The Armor of the Legend." *Rebels and Ancestors: The American Novel 1890–1915*. Boston: Houghton, Mifflin, 1953.

Godbold, E. Stanley, Jr. *Ellen Glasgow and the Woman Within*. Baton Rouge: Louisiana State University Press, 1972.

Gray, Richard. *The Literature of Memory: Modern Writers of the American South*. Baltimore: The Johns Hopkins Press, 1977.

Hardy, John Edward. "Ellen Glasgow." In *Southern Renascence: The Literature of the Modern South*. Ed. Louis D. Rubin, Jr., and Robert D. Jacobs. Baltimore: The Johns Hopkins Press, 1953.

Holman, C. Hugh. "Ellen Glasgow: The Novelist of Manners as Social Critic." *Three Modes of Southern Fiction: Ellen Glasgow, William Faulkner, Thomas Wolfe*. Athens: The University of Georgia Press, 1966.

———. "April in Queenborough: Ellen Glasgow's Comedies of Manners," "*Barren Ground* and the Shape of History." In *Windows on the World: Essays on Ameri-*

can Social Fiction. Knoxville: The University of Tennessee Press, 1979.

Inge, M. Thomas, ed., *Ellen Glasgow: Centennial Essays.* Charlottesville: University Press of Virginia, 1976.

Jessup, Josephine Lurie, *The Faith of Our Feminists: A Study in the Novels of Edith Wharton, Ellen Glasgow, Willa Cather.* New York: Richard R. Smith, 1950.

Jones, Anne Goodwyn. *Tomorrow is Another Day: The Woman Writer in the South, 1859–1936.* Baton Rouge: Louisiana State University Press, 1981.

Kazin, Alfred. "Elegy and Satire: Willa Cather and Ellen Glasgow." *On Native Grounds.* New York: Harcourt, Brace and Co., 1942.

––––––. "The Lost Rebel." *The Inmost Leaf.* New York: Harcourt, Brace, 1955.

Lawrence, Margaret. "Sophisticated Ladies: Ellen Glasgow." *The School of Femininity: A Book For and About Women as They Are Interpreted Through Feminine Writers of Yesterday and Today.* New York: Frederick A. Stokes Co., 1936.

MacDonald, Edgar E. "The Glasgow-Cabell Entente," *American Literature,* 41 (March 1969), 265–271.

––––––. (ed.). *The Ellen Glasgow Newsletter.* 1974– . Ashland, Virginia.

McDowell, Frederick P.W. *Ellen Glasgow and the Ironic Art of Fiction.* Madison: University of Wisconsin Press, 1960.

Mann, Dorothea Lawrance. *Ellen Glasgow.* Garden City, New York: Doubleday, Page & Co., 1927.

Marcosson, Isaac F. *Before I Forget: A Pilgrimage to the Past.* New York: Dodd, Mead Co., 1959.

Meade, Julian R. *I Live in Virginia.* New York: Longmans, Green and Co., 1935.

Mississippi Quarterly 31 (Winter, 1977–78). Special Section: "The Apprenticeship of Ellen Glasgow."

Mixon, Wayne. "Old Virginia and the New South Movement: The View From One West Main." *Southern Writers and The New South Movement. 1865–1913.* Chapel Hill: University of North Carolina Press, 1980.

Monroe, N. Elizabeth. "Ellen Glasgow: Ironist of Manners." *Fifty Years of the American Novel: A Christian Appraisal.* Ed. Harold C. Gardiner. New York: Charles Scribner's Sons, 1951.

Overton, Grant. "Ellen Glasgow." *The Women Who Make Our Novels.* Rev. ed. New York: Dodd, Mead, 1928.

Parent, Monique. *Ellen Glasgow: Romancière.* Paris: A. G. Nizet, 1962.

Raper, Julius Rowan. *Without Shelter: The Early Career of Ellen Glasgow.* Baton Rouge: Louisiana State University Press, 1971.

———. *From the Sunken Garden. The Fiction of Ellen Glasgow, 1916–1945.* Baton Rouge: Louisiana State University Press, 1980.

Rawlings, Marjorie Kinnan. "Regional Literature of the South." *College English,* 1 (February, 1940), 381–89.

Richards, Marion K. *Ellen Glasgow's Development as a Novelist.* The Hague: Mouton, 1971.

Rouse, Blair. *Ellen Glasgow.* Twayne United States Authors Series. New York: Twayne, 1962.

Rubin, Louis D., Jr. "Two in Richmond: Ellen Glasgow and James Branch Cabell." *The Curious Death of the Novel: Essays in American Literature.* Baton Rouge: Louisiana State University Press, 1967.

———. *No Place on Earth: Ellen Glasgow, James Branch Cabell, and Richmond-in-Virginia.* Austin: The University of Texas Press, 1959.

Santas, Joan Foster. *Ellen Glasgow's American Dream.* Charlottesville: The University Press of Virginia, 1965.

Sherman, Stuart, Sara Haardt, and Emily Clark. *Ellen Glasgow: Critical Essays.* New York: Doubleday, Doran, 1929.

Tutwiler, Carrington C., Jr. *A Catalogue of the Library of Ellen Glasgow.* Charlottesville: Bibliographical Society of the University of Virginia, 1969.

Wagenknecht, Edward. "Ellen Glasgow: Triumph and Despair." In *Cavalcade of the American Novel: From the Birth of the Nation to the Middle of the Twentieth Century.* New York: Henry Holt, 1952.

Index

217